DATE DUE

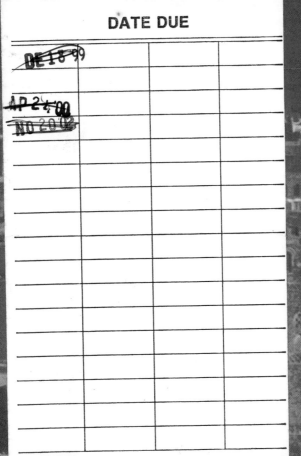

DE 18 99		
AP 27 00		
NO 20 02		

DEMCO 38-296

Old Sanaa with its high houses decorated with stucco lace rests against the Djebel Nogum (the Mountain of the Stars).

YEMEN

LAURENCE DEONNA
Translated by Corinne Borel

YEMEN

THREE CONTINENTS PRESS

Copyright © Laurence Deonna 1991

Translation by Corinne Borel
A Three Continents Book

Published in the United States of America by
Lynne Rienner Publishers, Inc.
1800 30th Street, Boulder, Colorado 80301

Copyright © by Fouad el-Foutaih,
Yemenite artist, of all drawings
in this volume; the rights to publish
herein granted to Laurence Deonna

Original French-language edition, 1982,
Editions 24 Heures, Lausanne (Switzerland), 1983, Editions Arthaud, Paris.
Poems by Abdel Aziz el-Maqali
and Mohamed al-Sharafi
were translated from the French into English
by Corinne Borel and
Laurence Deonna from
the work *Poèmes de la Révolution Yémenite*, Editions Recherches, Paris, 1979

Library of Congress Cataloging-in-Publication Data
Deonna, Laurence.
    Yemen / Laurence Deonna.
        p.   cm.
    ISBN 0-89410-710-0 (acid-free) : $24.00. — ISBN 0-89410-711-9
(pbk : acid-free) : $12.00
    1. Yemen—Description and travel.   I. Title.
DS247.Y42D45   1991   91-50116
953.3—dc20   CIP

Cover Art, Flap Copy
and Photographs
© Laurence Deonna, 1991

Cover Picture:
A wedding in Sanaa; the bride's girlfriends join in the festivities

To Farag

Contents

INTRODUCTION

A Few Traces of History

"This child thinks she's the queen of Sheba!" My father's voice sounded tender and warm. I was nine years old. My father smiled when he saw me appear in the doorway, a little terror, dressed up in a gown with a train and pearly slippers, mama's size.

In my mother's closet I also uncovered a necklace, earrings, gold bracelet and silver belt. From her drawer I pulled out the red that's smeared over my lips, the black dripping from my eyelashes, the blue running down my eyelids.

God, Allah, and my parents know very well that I am not a dream-child, although I dream a lot. I cut up rags from my new dresses and sell matches while it snows, just like the poor little girl in Andersen's fairytales. Today, covered in silk, I am the reincarnation of Titiana, the queen of fairies. Don't you see, Daddy, I'm not the queen of Sheba!

The queen of Sheba, don't know her! Well, a bit . . . The Bible says that she's a beautiful lady. King Solomon was in love with her. In a picture they are curled up together in a bed. A black slave fans them with feathers. Only their faces can be seen . . . What are they doing under the blanket? I think I know.

But how could my precocious knowledge tell me that years later I would actually visit the country said to be the legendary queen's?

It has been told that Bilkis, queen of Sheba, left her Yemenite kingdom to go visit King Solomon. She bedazzled him with her beauty, not to mention the cargo of her caravans: cloths, perfumes, spices, precious woods, rare goods from India, East Africa, the isles of the Indian ocean, Java, Sumatra, Ceylon, Malaya, Siam and China.

The history of Yemen is that of a thousand and one oblivions, although it is known that a thousand years before Jesus Christ or well before that, the ancient Yemenites already had all the secrets of the winds and the waves. Their great sailboats brought back from Asia treasures not to be found in the Near-East nor on the banks of the Mediterranean. At the same time Europeans were hunting wild ox in the depths of glacial forests. Working under the hot sun of the Orient caravans off-loaded from the boats onto the backs of camels, their long line stretching as far as the eye could see, to the very tip of the horizon winding north, and east into the lands of Hittites, the Medes, and the Assyrians.

This fruitful traffic over the centuries brought wealth to the lands of Sheba and its neighboring kingdoms. In awe of the palaces inlaid with ivory, silver and gold, dazzled by the sumptuous clothes decorated with ostrich feathers, intoxicated by the perfumes of myrrh and incense, the Greeks and the Romans were to call Yemen, *"Arabia Felix"* ("Happy Arabia"). To the tribes of the north who haunted the scorched sands, Yemen was "green Arabia," for true deserts are rare in Yemen where vertiginous mountains stand at dizzying heights and where most of its valleys and plains are fertile.

The land of Sheba also owed its prosperity to a colossal dam above Marib, the ancient capital. A work worthy of Hercules! Built by advanced techniques that foreshadowed modern times, the dam measured 1,969 feet in length, and some 197 feet at the base. Even today, its remains are impressive. The Koran, itself, written centuries later, says that "the inhabitants of the kingdom of Sheba relished not only one, but two Gardens of Eden: one on the right bank of the dam, the other on the left bank." Later, alas, when the dike had collapsed for the first time, the Book of the Prophet said: "There where lush gardens flourished was nothing more than arid earth where only bitter berries grew."

As the declining kingdom of the Sabeens was faced with the neighboring Himyarite kingdom's growing power, it also had to confront the new currents coming from the propagators of Jewish and Christian monotheism. These criss-crossed pagan Yemen, leading many local rulers to convert to monotheism, thus bringing about new power struggles.

Today, in Yemen, the tragic story of Dhou Nowas, called "the curly-headed one," is still evoked. This handsome Jewish king massacred Christians by the thousands. When he was eventually con-

During our Middle Ages, Arwa, a queen as prestigious in Yemen as the Queen of Sheba, lived in Djibla, one of the ancient capitals of Yemen.

quered by the Copts of Ethiopia, Christians from across the Red Sea, Dhou Nowas, mounted on his finest horse, committed suicide by riding off a cliff into the sea.

At the time, Mecca, where Mohammed had just been born, already was a magnet to mystics and intellectuals. Dhou Nowas's Christian successor would thereafter try in vain to evangelize neighboring Yemen. Discouraged by his missionary failure and military setbacks, the Christian King turned to the King of Persia who after much hesitation finally decided to give him aid. As is often the result of such invitations, the Yemenite Christian protege rapidly was demoted to being a subject, as the Persians extended their influence over the region. Yemen thereafter remained a province of the Persian Empire for many generations.

Located close to Mecca, Yemen was one of the first regions affected by the spread of Islam. The Arabic language soon followed. The schism between Sunnites, followers of Mohammed, and Shiites, devotees of his son-in-law Ali, has been strongly felt here from the very start.

At the beginning of the ninth century A.D., a new sect emerged in Mesopotamia (today's Iraq) from the Shiite Islamic doctrine: *Zaidism.* A few Yemenites departed their increasingly chaotic country and traveled to Mesopotamia. There they sought out a Zaidite, said to be one of Ali's descendants, begging him to come and bring order to Yemen. This is how El Hadi Yahia Ibn el-Hussein came to be the first King of Yemen, founding one of the longest dynasties in history. Today, under the Republic, his descendants are still considered the superior caste.

The Zaidite dynasty's power lapsed from time to time allowing various rival nobles to maintain their independence. The legendary queen Arwa, ruler of the region of Ibb and the princes of Zebid— a city near the Red Sea where the principles of algebra were discovered—were among these.

The fierce Zaidites, over the long run, however, knew how to maintain their power, whether defending their realm in battle, or, entrenched defensively in their mountains. They successfully resisted attempted invasions over the centuries by the armies of Saladin, of Ethiopian Copts, and by Christian Portuguese. Finally, the roof fell, the Turks occupying Yemen in 1528, to maintain their control for nearly a century, until Imam Qacim of Yemen at last drove them from his country.

Though the Turks returned two centuries later, in 1840, they would never be able totally to subdue the fierce Yemenites. The

Zaidite Imam's country at the tip of Arabia remained one of the Turkish Empire's most rebellious, so that the Turks' presence eventually became limited mainly to regions under rule of the *Shaffeites*, a sect born of the Islamic Sunni doctrine.

In 1839, the Aden and Hadramaut regions fell under the British mandate. One century later, in 1934, Yemen had three of its ancient provinces amputated: Asir, Jizan and Najran (which were ceded by Yemen's Imam to King Abdel Aziz of Saudi Arabia). This more recent loss is still deeply felt by Yemen.

Generation after generation the Yemenites have regaled their children with the great feats accomplished in 1905 by their king Imam Yahia. They recite how he freed his beloved city Sanaa from the Turks by launching bloody surprise raids, his shimmering sword challenging their thundering guns and cannons. Years later, in 1918, the Ottoman Empire was finally defeated by the combined Arab and British armies, and Yemen regained its independence.

Yemen joined the League of Nations and the Arab League early on. In one of history's ironies, this feudal country would even be one of the first to recognize the Soviet Union. But Imam Yahia, a conservative, terrified of foreign poisons, would avoid most international contacts as much as possible: "We prefer to live in poverty than to be rich and see our country under the boot of foreigners." To a Lebanese arms dealer seeking to sell him fighter planes he allegedly replied, brandishing the sacred book, "Don't need them! the Koran is all I need to shoot down enemy planes!"

Assassinated in 1948 by one of his relatives, Yahia was replaced by his son Ahmed "the Sword of Islam." Ahmed was the last symbol of another time, the last stitch in the tapestry of Yemen's ancient history. Then came the Revolution.

Thus the little girl who dreamed herself into the role of the queen of Sheba went in search of a "real" Yemen. This is the Yemen she saw, the photographs she took, the Yemenites she met, the secrets they confided in her. She has chosen to emphasize her personal impressions and the anecdotes she gathered during her sojourns.

Leaving objectivity to her camera, the voyager grants herself subjective license to better share with her readers the pulse of Yemen, something neither official documents, nor labored analyses, can render.

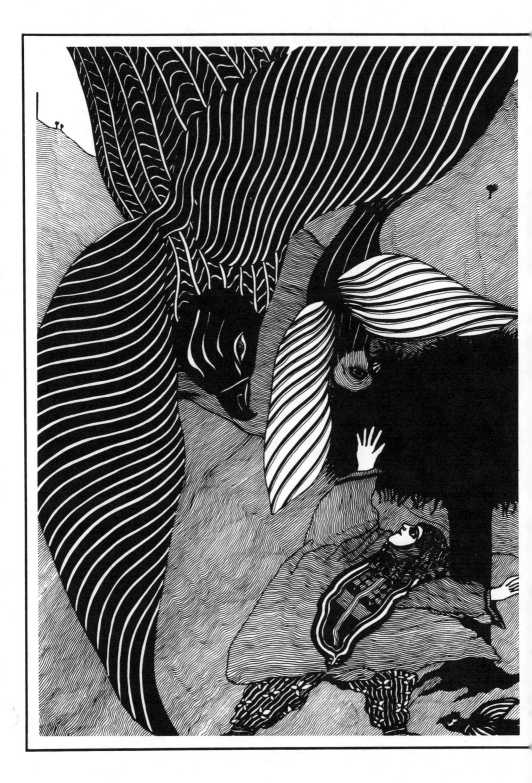

CHAPTER ONE

Epilogue for an All Too Picturesque Imam

To help the people "remember," the deeds of Imam Ahmed, the last potentate of Yemen, are staged today in one of his Taiz palaces (the Imam owned three in this city and five in Sanaa). In 1962 the tyrant had died in this beautiful place, the walls dressed in a stucco lace and flanked with multicolored mousharabiehs* in the Yemenite style. Ending a life of pomp and power, he endured a long agony after revolutionary bullets had punched eight holes in his body.

The palace has now been transformed into a museum by the Republic. Its flea market-like display could be entitled: "Panoramic view of the good life of a king whose people lived in misery." There isn't a detail, not a single object, missing. Here, unwinding before my eyes, is the "memory" of a despot who claimed to be vested with God's will and Divine right.

How enormous the chains which paralyzed the prisoners! How horrible the pictures where large sabers, caked with blood, slash. One placard reads: "Dear visitor, these photos show the heads of martyrs falling like those of lambs."

Among the executed were the "liberals," the idealists who had tried to free Yemen from the royal yoke. They failed twice, once in 1948 and again in 1955. Only after the death of Imam Ahmed in 1962 would the winds turn in their favor. Overthrown by the revolutionaries on September 26 of that same year—a date highlighted in Yemenite school books—Ahmed's son Al-Badr was allowed a reign of six days! And already the cry had gone up, "Vive la Republique!" Too soon in the event . . . Al-Badr, disguised as a woman, was able to flee to the north. He rallied the faithful tribes, called on the support of Saudi Arabia, and launched an attack on the devil's cohorts, those republicans! The civil war was to last eight years, and it has not yet ended the Yemenites' pain and anguish.

In Taiz museum, all the King's belongings, down to his socks, glasses and dentures, are on display. Nothing has been forgotten. Not his collection of watches, clocks or jewelry, nor, it's important to note, the luxury of a hairdryer, washing machine or electric stove, for until the Revolution in Yemen, only a few privileged ones in Taiz and Sanaa had had the benefits of electricity.

The show at the toy department of the museum consists of the presents the tyrant gave to his "darling boy": dolls, tops, a tricycle, a rocking horse, and a lifesize plush lion. "At night, the king brought it out to scare people!" a guard remembers.

The Imam cared little for the well being of his people, but he cared much for himself. He anointed himself with a debauchery of salves and balsams and swallowed pills, vitamins and fortifiers by the dozens. In the museum his multicolored perfumes are lined up in huge bottles of all shapes. The King had them special-ordered from Switzerland. He also had essences soaked in cow horns for months, the old-fashioned way.

His eyes always made up in *khol,* this oriental Narcissus enjoyed admiring himself in the many mirrors decorating his palace. His intense gaze gave him the name "Ahmed the Djinn" or "Ahmed the Demon." One of the legends which he himself propagated, had it that he was protected by spirits and that bullets would bounce off his body without wounding him.

A Puritanism That Even Calvin Would Find Excessive

In order to preserve a spotless Islam, the Imam prohibited his subjects from singing or dancing in public, except when they danced before the King himself and his family. And woe to he who would cock an ear to music, and above all to foreign ideas! Except for the King, the foreign waves would halt at the mountains of Yemen.

The people were completely isolated and the Imam was the only interpreter of the outer world. The tyrant possessed records, a gramophone, a tape recorder, which he hid under a cushion on his sofa during the visits of visitors. He encouraged them to talk, he provoked them to open up, then later he threatened them: "Listen, the djinns (devils) speak through your mouths . . ." Ahmed also owned a powerful radio which enabled him to expand on his legendary reputation: "I converse with spirits: They have informed me of the subversive talk of those revolutionary Yemenites holed up in Cairo!"

As that time, in Egypt, Gamal Abdel Nasser had carried out his own revolution. He had received the "liberal" Yemenites with great enthusiasm, and a few years later, fighting alongside them in Yemen under the republican flag, he would be entrenched in a five year war (1962–1967). The Egyptians had the planes but the royalists under the flag of the Imam had the mountains, and Nasser's troops were worn out by the conflict in this forsaken place. Weakened, they had their most stinging defeat elsewhere, in June 1967, losing on their own territory against the Israeli army.

Ironically, before backing the Yemenite Revolution, Nasser's visions of grandeur for a united Arab world had driven him to court Ahmed of Yemen, the most backward of monarchs. Nasser had seen Yemen as having a unique strategic position, and, in 1958, in Damascus, his efforts produced a federated union of Syria, Egypt and Yemen. Little came of it, however, and the union was dissolved in 1961. "Nasser is a rocking boat, overloaded with unrestrained hungers," wrote King Ahmed one day, for, he, like so many Yemenites, was also a poet and could discuss power and strife in vivid ways.

But the king also, as noted, had his appetites . . . and thirsts. He didn't neglect alcohol either. At the museum-palace sit, row on row, his unopened bottles of golden whiskey, of transparent Ouzo and regiments of soda water. The Imam, who on his subjects imposed a puritanism which even extremists would deem excessive, was himself beyond the reach of reproach. He would not have to risk the supreme Koranic humiliation: on being found guilty, an alcohol-drinker was paraded through the city, holding the offending flask on his head with both hands. Struggling down the street, with a huge drum attached to his back, the wretch would feel the vibrations of the drummer-of-the-day pounding, full force, alerting the people to this great shame.

Forty Years Spent in the Shadow of "Ahmed the Djinn"

The museum of Taiz also has his guide: El Hadj Ali el-Matari of the Bani Matar tribe. Eighty-seven years old when I met him! He wore a turban like a halo and a transparent gaze. He was a living memory.

"One day the Imam had drunk too much. He grabbed an officer by the sleeve: "Bring me a bunch of figs"—They're not in season—"Lies!" screamed the King, grabbing his sword, "I can do anything! If I wanted to I could turn you into a fig!" Hearing these words a nearby soldier fled, terrified."

The old Ali laughs,

"Think about it! The soldier must have said to himself: if the King could turn an officer into a fig, what would he do to me, a mere private!"".

In Yemen at the time this was no joke. For everyday people, the Imam was vested with God's will and you just could not escape his threats.

Long before, el Hadj Ali el-Matari had once been a soldier:

"Once a year, at the time of the Ramadan, the Imam would give us a new uniform: one skirt, a jacket, a shirt and a piece of cloth which we would use as both a cape and a blanket."

The King of Yemen's men didn't have shoes; summer and winter they went barefoot.

At the beginning of his military career in Imam Yahia's time, Ali earned five rials a month. As a veteran forty years later, under the reign of Ahmed, he barely earned any more: seven and a half rials. A private had no choice but to submit. "In those times we didn't dare complain! And if we complained . . ."

The guide signals me to follow. He hobbles, stops, and points his walking stick to a ribbon of stained yellow paper, hanging from the ceiling to the ground where it snakes around.

"These are letters glued from one end to the other. Three yards of bureaucracy: years of correspondence, years of pleas. For nothing! A yoyo of requests and refusals between a soldier who begged for a raise and the Imam who took pleasure in refusing him. And you'll never guess what was at stake in all these papers? A quarter rial!"

What else could any poor soldier do, but write to the Imam? There was no one else but the Imam. The King decided all, for all, weighed the least of details and even opened all of the palace mail himself. And, there was no way to appeal his judgement.

The museum-palace is an exhausting labyrinth. Ali grumbles going up and down a succession of spiraling stairs. He shamelessly seats his commoner's behind on one of the royal beds. Don't imagine plush pillows or exquisite silk rugs. Set next to a dentist's chair, this is a hospital bed: an Assassinated-Imam's-Death-Bed.

I am from the land of quat
Miseries weigh heavy.
I am a sad song,
A letter from exile.
Above angry volcanoes,
I escaped the prison of the past,
Chains crimping my wrists,
Exhaustion bowing my legs
I carry no perfumes.
My desert has no oil,
And I have no gold.

Abdel Aziz el-Maqali

Detail of a painting by Yemenite artist, Abdeljabbar Noman

Wounded, the King used the electric controls to adjust his position, hoping to alleviate his pain.

The guide squints his eyes, their color faded by the impressions of a very long life:

"I saw the Imam the day of his death. He was like an egg all pale and yellow, he dragged himself from one door to the next. He collapsed on his bed."

Old people's memories often color and soften the past.

"He was a good king," murmurs Ali. But he sees further. He concentrates. He relives "the good old days"—which after all, were not so good. He remembers those years spent in the shadow of "Ahmed the Djinn", a demon with a formidable beard reddened by henna:

"At the beginning I really liked him. But little by little I understood. Each day I was a little more scared. In the end it was awful with those eyes of his glaring out everywhere! rolling, rolling . . ."

The Palace's Drugstore

Morphine was what had made the King's eyes "roll." The quacks and doctors surrounding him prescribed it, coming from all over to treat him. They rivaled each other, seeking new, ingenious ways to maintain their influence on the King. Some intoxicated themselves, not with morphine, but with the hope of royal favors and the possibility of business deals on the side.

And while each drugged himself, and the King, each in his own way, the common people were left to perish. It still infuriates old Ali:

"All those foreign drugs were for the King and his entourage. Outside this privileged circle his generosity would depend on his mood. A life-saving pill would be denied those he didn't like. A member of the great Iriani family had to go down the mountains, take a boat, cross the Red Sea, and get himself all the way to Ethiopia to get penicillin, which Ahmed could have simply given him. It cost him a fortune: one thousand rials!"

Until the unenlightened despot's death only one hospital had been built, in Hodeyda, a port on the Red Sea modernized by the Soviets. There were no roads to it from the rest of the country except for a short strip built by the Chinese between Hodeyda and Sanaa, the capital. The first thing the Republicans had to worry about at the end of the civil war was dealing with this disastrous situation. Today one can find medical services in many large villages, not to mention clinics built by the Russians, Chinese, Swedes, Germans, Kuwaitis, and others.

"Keep Your Dog Hungry, He'll Follow You"

There are many visitors now to the palace of Taiz: young men, women, families. Charming old patriarchs take a journey through the museum and their memories. One of these pilgrims is old Mohammed. I can see him standing, frozen in his tracks, in awe before the huge fringed parasol that a slave once carried to shade His Sacred Majesty. Between the worn turban and the snow-white beard blinks a keen, if myopic, gaze: Mohammed is an intellectual. In pioneering days he was one of the very few teachers in Yemen.

"Non-religious books had to be brought into Yemen secretly. I had to scheme and come up with all kinds of tricks to make myself a small library. These books came from Egypt or Aden where, thanks to the British, minds began to open up. But the Imam found my books! He was furious and confiscated my library, threatening to imprison me: 'Mohammed, don't forget that a revolution in thought ends with a revolution in blood!' "

Indeed, accurate words: the King, no fool, was cultured, intelligent, an artist and, especially, a poet.

"But he wanted us to remain archaic for all eternity, forever living in poverty. 'Keep your dog hungry, he'll follow you!': King Ahmed observed this precept to the letter. He made sure that no one, not even in his private circle, bettered himself. Luxury was only for him!"

Mohammed recalls an example he finds particularly enlightening:

"One day, a man arrived at the palace, beautifully dressed, all embroidered in silver. The Imam scrutinized every detail from top to bottom, commenting sarcastically on the cloth's decorations, making fun of his subject's pretentions to the point where the man left, confused and humiliated. After this scenario repeated itself several times, the poor man finally decided to sell his fine suit."

Professor Mohammed's comments get the people around us all excited. They press up against us. The royal parasol is jostled. Each is dying to give his own little contribution to History.

"Right in the middle of a famine, the King ordered that sacks of wheat be burned!"

"Whoever couldn't pay the King's taxes had to sell his possessions."

"He took the son of our tribe's chief as a hostage, a six year old child, and kept him prisoner in a fortress for years."

"He wanted to control everything. In 1955, when he received the tanks bought from the Soviets, he put them in a shed at military headquarters and kept the keys to himself."

"In 1948 after the first coup and the death of Imam Yahia, Ahmed the new king fled to Saudi Arabia. When he met the northern tribes, rebels to his authority but easy to buy off, and fanatics of Islam, he cried 'Revolution is the devil's work!' The tribes rallied around him, a real horde of Mongols. Ahmed won, for a time. He beheaded many."

The storyteller wipes his brow:

"I can still see the survivors: three hundred revolutionaries in rags, chained, dragging their bare feet on the stones, the sun pounding on them. They crossed a third of Yemen, from the city of Dhamar, south of Sanaa, all the way to the Hajja prison in the north. In this isolated fortress perched on the rocks, the Imam locked up his political prisoners."

The man grows frenzied.

"The prison of Hajja was a cauldron of revolt where the most revolutionary ideas were fermenting. The craziest dreams grew there. Between the men in dungeons and their free accomplices, the news traveled mysteriously, crossed the thickest walls, went from valley to valley, from mountain to mountain. The message penetrated to the country's horizons and broke through the borders."

In 1955 after another failed uprising, King Ahmed decided to behead two of his brothers, Ibrahim and Abdallah. Ibrahim, particularly, was very popular among the Yemenite people and was called "The Sword of Righteousness."

A Piece of the Moon at the Medieval Museum of Sanaa

Shimmering royal swords decorate a towering room in Dar el-Shukr palace, made into Sanaa's National Museum. They lie near spectacular curved daggers ("jambias") and heavy muskets inlaid with silver. A crowd of turbaned men walk by these antiques, their sidearms laid against their stomachs. "In every Yemenite runs the blood of a warrior" says the proverb and the men have a lively response to this martial display.

Pages of the royal family album are laid open in the next room.

Frozen eternally on withered photographs are three generations of Imams still scoffing at the good people: Yahia, Ahmed and Al-Badr. Their beards are all they have in common. One has a cruel look, the second hypnotic eyes, the third a dull gaze. By al-Badr's well fed face one can see that Allah, so stingy with the Yemenites' poor, showed himself generous to the descendants of divine Mohammed's son-in-law, Ali. A sign of nobility: the Imams wear their daggers on the right side slipped into magnificently decorated belts.

One of the visitors, furiously gripping his "jambia," insults the royal portraits under his breath:

"You treated us like objects, you kept us blind!"

The official gifts given to the Imam's successors, the leaders of modern Yemen, are gathered in another room. France, responding to Yemen's tastes, presented a small, over-decorated antique revolver. Iraq distinguished itself with a magnificent sabre. Syria, obsessed with Israel, came up with a cheap candy box embellished with a photo of Kuneitra, the Syrian city which at that time was under Zionist occupation.

Ibrahim Hamdi, the Yemenite chief-of-state from 1974 to 1977, gave his personal donation to the historical museum: a stuffed mongoose swallowing a stuffed snake. Hamdi was very popular with his people, not only for his democratic spirit . . . but, also, *because he observed traffic lights.* Yes, that's all true!

A bunch of visitors cluster around a display table. These are village men who have descended from the mountains where there is no electricity and women still go to wells the way they did a thousand years ago. Clanking against each other's daggers, they bend over the flat panes of glass. Under the smeared cover rests a small black stone. It's a piece of the moon brought back to earth by American astronauts.

A sign announces: "Given to the people of Yemen by Richard Nixon, President of the United States of America." Nearby, next to a somewhat ragged flag of Yemen, another inscription reads: "The flag of your country was carried to the moon aboard the spaceship AMERICA during the Apollo XVII mission, December 7–9, 1972."

Egyptian Veterans of the Yemenite War Remember

Tourists and veterans alike make sure not to miss a visit to this museum.

"I am fifty years old, and Egyptian, a retired officer. Two years of war in Yemen. God it was tough. It was 1964 . . . a thousand years ago . . . Today, when I see what has become of Sanaa, its cars, its traffic, its boutiques, its neon lights, I think I'm dreaming."

Nabil is in Yemen not to stir up his memories, but to pay a visit to his son, an instructor in a nearby school. Egyptians teach as far as the most remote hamlets. One peasant said to me, with that sense of terse metaphor Yemenites are so gifted for:

"In the old days we shared the trenches with the Egyptians, battling against the Royalists. Today we share the trenches with them, battling against ignorance".

A Yemenite bystander leaning his ear towards us adds:

"These Egyptian teachers, doctors and specialists are important. Hopefully they'll continue to bring us the weight of their knowledge, and even their round bellies. But for God's sake let them leave the weight of their bureaucracy at home."

Nabil, a former officer of Nasser, has left behind his military uniform for the classic Egyptian civilian uniform: a V-neck sweater, a belt below the belly, pants waving around generous curves. Legs apart, hands on hips, he stretches his round bald head fringed with scant curly hair towards the large chicken wire cage, set in the museum's courtyard. The cage is walled off on three sides. What's hiding in the dark? A monkey? A lion? A forgotten prisoner?

"The Imam's carriage!" an approaching passerby tells me, laughing. "Believe me, for the Yemenite people not so long ago, this old cart was considered a Sputnick!"

"Its true," blurts out Nabil, "the poor fellows lived on another planet. Once you had crossed Yemen's border you had no choice but to submit yourself to the whims of the King. Even foreign journalists. In 1961 the Imam sent a message to Cairo: 'I want the representatives of the Egyptian press to come see me.' "

A royal whim was an order. The journalists boarded a plane, flew over the Red Sea, set foot on Yemenite ground . . . and were immediately surrounded by the Imam's guards, armed to the teeth.

Nabil shrugs:

"They had no choice but to obey! The Egyptians were kept prisoners until Ahmed deemed to receive them. A day passed, then two: not a sign from the palace. The third night the Imam finally informed the journalists of his decision: he would not see them. His Majesty had changed his mind. Ahmed's guests were brought back to the airport. They were not to see the King, nor Yemen, nor did they catch a glimpse of the capital."

Nasser's former officer doubles over laughing.

"A few weeks later, a porter dropped off a six foot long sack in front of the Cairo Press Office. It was a 165 pound bag of coffee. 'With his apologies, His Majesty sends a sample of Yemen's main produce . . .' "

When he speaks of the Yemenites Nabil is both tender and a bit patronizing.

"It was during the war. Our pilots needed a landing strip. After having found a site and brought over workers from Egypt we went to work. We were starting to lay the asphalt when some men came running over to us, wildly waving their hands, threatening us: 'Who gave you the right to touch the earth which God created! Who gave you the right to change it!' "

Sealed off from the modern world by their Imam, their religion and their mountains, many Yemenites held a sacred respect for all divine creation.

The Voice of Nasser

Though they are superstitious, the Yemenites have always been redoubtable warriors. In five years of vicious fighting, Egypt lost thousands of men in the Republic's cause. Left to themselves after the departure of Nasser's troops in 1967, Republicans would not give up the struggle. Nor would the Royalists.

Victory was finally attained for the Republicans by a hair's breadth. In 1970 they found themselves head of an exhausted country, weakened all the more by the Sheikhs's political maneuvers. Throughout the war, selling themselves to the highest bidder, these tribal chiefs, traditionally against all centralized power, shifted between the enemy brothers, Royalists or Republicans.

Some Yemenites now criticize the Egyptians for having gone to Yemen as conquerors; others admit that the Yemenites only won freedom because of the sacrifices of Nasser's army.

For a long time the Nasser cult was alive and well in Yemen. Some strong images come back to me. In Taiz, in the window of the "Revolutionary Conscience Bookshop," Nasser's king-sized portrait sat next to a pint-sized one of the President of the Republic. Nasser's form was also on the dark wall of the "Tailor of Freedom" shop, where the poor tailor pumped the sewing machine pedal day and night, in hopes of one day reaching democracy. At the "House of the People" barber shop, Nasser scoffed from the heights of his picture frame at the barber's customers fluffed up with foam and slouched over in their seats.

Shrewd vendors did good business selling his well-known voice on tape along with Arab flute melodies and the beat of rock.

In the hearts of many Yemenites a memory is still held dear: the President of Egypt's visit, the only one he ever made to Yemen. It was in Taiz in 1964. Facing an immense, electrified crowd, Nasser's voice resonated between the high mountains underneath a scorching sun.

"Brothers, if the British refuse to leave Aden, we will be the ones to oust them."

This dramatic speech would inspire Yemenites from the South to get organized militarily and to begin serious training.

The Country Is Torn Apart—
Southern Yemen Creates Its Own State

While the northern regions of Yemen plunged into civil war, the southern area, under British domination since 1839, undertook a gradual transformation more profound than the north's.

The south opened onto the ocean and so onto avant-garde ideologies. The most politically subversive ideas would spring from Taiz, a city relatively close to the British protectorate. Taiz was the cradle of the Southern Yemen Liberation Front. But this Front was not radical enough for the new party, even more nationalist and progressive, the National Liberation Front (NLF). Eventually the NLF took over, winning the Revolution.

In 1967 the NLF, after the departure of the last British soldier, proclaimed the region around Aden as the Popular Republic of Yemen. In 1970 the party's extreme left-wing would transform it into the People's Democratic Republic of Yemen and link itself with the Soviet Union and the Eastern Bloc.

From then on, oil rich Saudi Arabia, which considered communism satanic, had no choice but to become the patron-daddy of the northern part of Yemen. Northern Yemen had indeed become a fragile buffer state between the most traditional country of the peninsula, Saudi Arabia, and the revolutionary People's Democratic Republic of Yemen in the South.

For a long time Sanaa, the North's capital, would euphemistically call communist Yemen "the homeland's south" . . .

So for nearly a quarter century, two Yemens would exist. Northern Yemen, where the impressions and images of this book take

place, was called The Arab Republic of Yemen (capital, Sanaa). Southern Yemen was to take the name The People's Democratic Republic of Yemen (capital, Aden). In these two countries living side by side, Islam and communism like oil and water, would never blend.

"My wallet is in the North but my heart is in the South," a young man confided to me in the Sanaa post office.

The poor boy was going out of his mind. He had been trying for hours to get Aden by phone. It was the third full day of his efforts.

"I have no news. It's been over a week since my wife left to give birth at her mother's in Aden. My mother-in-law wouldn't have been able to come to Sanaa because you have to fill out hundreds of forms and leave a large deposit there. Do you know that every Yemenite, North and South, has a father, mother, brother, uncle, or cousin 'on the other side'?"

1990: The Two Yemens Become a Single State

Since their separation, the two Yemens have always lived not only apart, but teetering between war and peace. Twice, in 1972 and again in 1979, their latent conflict exploded into violent battles. In 1986 a civil war ravaged Aden, forcing thousands of refugees to flee to Northern Yemen. Sanaa welcomed them as brothers, granting them all citizens' rights.

Has this human element played its role in the reunification or is the union of the two Yemens only due to politics—and high politics? Yet the miracle did occur. This union dreamed about for so many years, unceasingly talked about again and again by bi-partisan commissions, was finally attained May 22, 1990.

A new Constitution bonds the two countries, now simply called The Republic of Yemen. A new Parliament has been established with 159 deputies from the North and 142 from the South, making a total of 301 deputies. The new Government has 38 Ministers, 22 from the South and 16 from the North. A Presidential Council of five members was elected. Its Chairman was General Ali Abdullah Saleh, from the North, and its Vice-Chairman Mr. Ali Salem el-Bid, from the South. Both men keeping their position as Secretary General of their own leading party.

Sanaa, the point of departure and return for my journeys across Yemen, will from now on be the political capital of the new State while Aden will be its economic capital.

What can be said about this marriage? And what will become of its children? How will the "enemy brothers" of yesterday live out their reconciliation?

Only time will tell . . .

Remember though, that Yemenites adapt easily to new situa-

During the Revolution women carried shells on their heads the way other women carry their laundry to the river.

tions whatever they may be. Haven't I met people in the country's north who've never learned how to write and were propelled with no transition into the jet age, seemingly unperturbed?

In my opinion nothing, nor anyone, is capable of really surprising a Yemenite.

CHAPTER TWO

The Koran on the Tube, Minstrels on Tape

P raise be to God! The evenings of traditional poetry are broadcast on radio and television."

El Issi Moussawai rejoices ecstatically. He is a minstrel in front of God, lackey of flattery in front of the government, lyrical in front of me.

The poet, a man in his 60s, directs the Ministry of Information and Culture Bureau in the port of Hodeyda. The city sprouts up modern and busy on the Red Sea.

At dawn, I visited its old quarters. It was dawn and yet it felt like dusk. Up against the sea and progress, its ancient Turkish palaces were collapsing. Behind the torn lacework of their wooden moucharabiehs were only the dead stares of ghosts. Except for the moaning of invisible pigeons, all was silence. A light sea-scented wind drifted through the gutted walls.

The minstrel's window looks out onto a parched garden and rows of houses eaten away by salt. Further away one can make out the sea. One can smell its scent but its dances remain hidden. A typical Yemenite curtain hides another window. The curtain consists of two poorly-hung pieces of fabric, pinned on either side like puppet theatre curtains and overhung clumsily by a board covered with the same fabric. Behind his chair the poet has enthroned a magnificent stereo/tape player—and a portrait of the President of the Republic.

On the "Artist-Director's" table—ornamented with violet felt—a few dusty official papers lay forgotten. El Issi Moussawai is a fake *23* bureaucrat but a genuine poet. Not even giving me a chance to sit down, he launches his monologue.

"Be welcome and listen! Last night in the sweetness of the night, I composed 80 verses," he proclaims in a loud voice. His brow furrows, his eyes open up, his hands stir the hot, humid air.

"I speak of the dark years before the arrival of the Prophet. I lament the oppression of the Arabs in a world divided between two great powers, the Persians to the East and the Romans to the West."

I interrupt the poet's enthusiasm and ask:

"Today it's the Russians and the Americans isn't it?"

Thrilled, the artist applauds. His large dark face radiates beneath his white skullcap. We've become friends. In this world of metaphor I've gained his respect by leaving behind the cumbersome shoes of the West for the graceful sandals of arabesque and symbol.

El Issi Moussawai continues,

"At that time the Arabs were strong, the Prophet had unified His empire through faith. Today, faith melts like butter in the sun. Today, fragile birds that we are, we're caught in the nets of fowlers and those who sell us talons."

With this powerful image the poet rises, readjusts his skullcap and goes to kneel toward Mecca to recite the noon prayer. He returns. I'm impatient.

"So what about these evenings of poetry?"

"It's an old custom which is still alive. Poetry was one of the few forms of entertainment allowed by the Imam. Yemenites have it in their blood. At our Writer's Association of Hodeyda, poets submit their works a few of which are selected for the evening's poetry reading. Usually each poet recites one or two poems, no more, unless the crowd begs him to go on."

Sometimes the beauty of a verse gives chills to the audience. Sometimes the topic of a poem inspires passions, leading to endless debates and unceasing discussions which go on for weeks on the streets, in the marketplace, in homes, anywhere, anytime.

The versifiers tell of the traditional, social and political life of Yemen. Of course they laud the Revolution.

"But no glorifying of the Chief-of-State," insists El Issi Moussawai, who wants to preserve his image as a free, if not liberated, artist. "No love poems either, Yemenites are too hot-blooded!"

So what has become of you, o voluptuousness, o perfidy? What has become of you, long black mane the color of night, eyes of a gazelle, lips tasting like wine? Where have you gone, troubadours of my thousand and one mirages? And why such austerity when Yemen is supposedly opening itself to the world and its pleasures?

In the evening poetry readings, the outrageous price of a bride is lamented in verse. Marrying daughters is a lucrative business for heads of families, a veritable gold mine.

"But I thought a limit had been set by law," I say, "and that going beyond that amount was illegal?"

The old troubadour laughs with every wrinkle. He opens his hands in a gesture of resignation:

"You're right! Alas, our fine Yemen isn't America . . ."

Today's high cost of living also finds its way into sobbing lyrics. But have Yemenites already forgotten yesterday's true misery? El Issi Moussawai leans back in his chair.

"I wrote these verses a long long time ago.

> *If you ask a poor man, 'Are you hungry?'*
> *He will veil his face.*
> *But look him straight in the eye*
> *And you will see revolt raging*

The poet becomes fiery.

"Yes! The starving Yemenite people revolted while the Imam was dreaming, seated on his pillow of power. Just like that Marie-Antoinette! The hungry French demanded bread from her. 'You have no bread? Then have some cake!' replied the queen. Wallahi! The people took her cake, her bread . . . and her head!"

I broach a naive question, which actually isn't so naive:

"And quat*? Do you praise or condemn it?"

El Issi Moussawai takes on the air of a wiseman who's come to peace with his contradictions:

"I do condemn it a bit . . . Quat is like love: you love that gift of heavenly happiness, but you hate the knife of weakness driven into your guts."

The meeting between the Yemenite troubadour and the journalist takes an unexpected turn. We are like two children telling each other stories, exchanging tales of East and West. One of them written by the Danish fabulist Andersen, stupefies our Arabian poet. What? A princess who can feel a little pea through layers of mattresses? He's never heard of such a thing, even of the finest princes, even of the Court of Haroun el-Rachid The Great!

But my guide interrupts. Enough princes and princesses! I pick up my notebook, put on my hat, and off we go again on the roads of Arabia.

Before starting out, hoping to please him, I tell the director-poet of Hodeyda how much I love the volcanic rocks that run like veins through Yemen . . . the arid lands . . . the desert . . .

The troubadour casts a sharp glance at my rosy cheeks, the cheeks of a child from lush green lands, and with these words he reminds me to be more discreet in my attempts to be original.

"My dear, many wearing silk clothes pretend they dream of sleeping on a hard mat . . ."

Leaving the shade for the sun and the modest office for the aging Mercedes, I leave my dear storyteller to his wisdom and nostalgia. In the stairway, my guide stops suddenly.

"That's all fine: the past, the stories, the princes, the kings! But what the true, great Yemenite poets celebrate is the Revolution!"

"Only praises?" I ask. "Never any criticism? Never just a touch of irony?

The young man smiles.

"Listen, these kinds of poems are only heard among us. We don't print them!"

From the Ottoman Gazette to the Revolution's Daily

The surprises of Yemen! Sanaa, enclosed within its walls and archaicness, is where the Arabian Peninsula's first newspaper, *Sanaa*, was created in 1879. Printed in Turkish and Arabic, this gazette was meant for the few existing literates. It disappeared in 1918 along with the Ottoman Empire.

Years passed.

In their Aden protectorate the British finally allowed the Yemenites to publish their *Fatat el-Gezira* ('Young Girl of the Peninsula') in 1940, the beginning of World War II. Allegedly the British hoped to manipulate this innocent Arab "girl" and use the medium for spreading a favorable image of themselves.

From 1944 on, the "liberal" Yemenites's medium, *Saut el-Yemen* (The Voice of Yemen) fanned the flames of revolt. Printed first in Aden then in Cairo, the revolutionary flyer managed to wind its way as far north as the mountains, all the way to the land of the iron-fisted Imam Yahia. *The Voice of Yemen* was mainly the voice of its editor-in-chief, the poet Ahmed el-Zoubeiri, soul and song of the Yemenite people. Both lyrical and militant, the paper's writers urged the building of roads, schools and hospitals. Abroad, this revolutionary voice was spread thanks to emigrants' publications,

In Sanaa, at the newspaper stalls, you not only find journals but also posters and pious images. The beauty of the image often takes precedence over the subject. Even the Blessed Virgin finds herself on neighboring terms with the Muslim Mecca.

such as the *El Salem* newspaper printed in Cardiff, Wales, by the Yemenite community of Great Britain.

"In the old days, only aristocrats and religious men knew how to write and with such beauty, such fine style! Since the Revolution, language has paled and lost its vigor," laments an old, white-bearded scholar.

Learn, O Very Venerable One, that alas, this is the price of democracy. Beautiful language is disappearing everywhere in the West . . .

In more recent times in Yemen many magazines sprang up, then quickly withered and died. They were piled, one on the other, at the corner newsstands. Foreign magazines in English were sometimes clipped of pages on the way from New York or London to Sanaa by mysterious scissors. The local dailies were at times splotched with the white strips of censorship.

The Ministry of Information in Sanaa publishes *Al Thawra* ("The Revolution"), a daily with a wide circulation. *Al Joumbourieh* ("The Republic"), a smaller daily, is a by-product of "The Revolution" and is printed in Taiz.

I met Mohammed el-Zarka in 1977, a small man with lively eyes and a percolating mind. He was then editor-in-chief of *The Revolution*.

"I don't know English. I don't have any other sources for reporting international politics but the telex from Beirut and Cairo. For more reliability I listen to the BBC in Arabic. That's all, but I manage. A good journalist has to be imaginative!"

He took it back. "Well, not too much . . ."

"How old are you?"

"Thirty-nine. But here in Yemen you age fast as a journalist . . ."

"The Revolution" tries very hard to correct "bad habits." It campaigns against the marketing of marriage and quat speculation. It wars against those who pile garbage into towers throughout the city, or pave streets in tin cans. In Yemen, alas, the consumers are winning the race against the trash collectors.

Radio Reaches Planet Yemen

1946. World War II is over. Germany is in ruins. Europe bled white. Skeletons and ghosts have emerged from the death camps. In Hiroshima, the Japanese have been stunned by the atomic age.

Journalist Mohamed El-Zarka—then editor-in-chief of "Al-Thawra", the Sanaa daily—snowed under with news . . .

The Yemenite people knew nothing of these horrors. They lived on the moon, sequestered in complete ignorance. Their world ended at the Red Sea which the all powerful Imam emptied and filled at his whim—so they thought.

Beyond the waves was nothingness . . .

Then it happened, the fabulous gift arrived! An American army truck, coming from the port of Djeddah, Saudi Arabia, finally made its entry through the gates of Sanaa, after having bumped along for days on the road between Hodeyda and the capital. It carried a mysterious object in its stomach, a radio transmitter plugged into the engine's battery.

And so, Radio-Sanaa was born. For a long time Eisenhower's army truck would be Sanaa's only transmission site.

This brand new station only reached a few dozen people, who being in the King's private circle, owned a radio. Yemen thus became the only country in the world where the radio didn't go to the listeners, but the listeners rushed to the radio. Broadcasts took place three times a week and lasted half an hour.

The radio, what a sight to see! Such crowds around the truck from America. One, two! One two! The Imam's drummers and trumpet players left guard duty for their stint in front of the microphone. The program opened and closed with their serenades. In between, the highlight of the show: a reading from the Koran.

North Yemen didn't have a real radio station until 1955. Before the Revolution, Radio-Sanaa, the only station authorized by the King, broadcast nothing but sermons, military marches and the acts and deeds of the Imam to saturation point. This could explain why today's Yemenites have an insatiable appetite for education, culture, news and music from all over the world. Radio, T.V., films and video; they never tire of it.

One of Radio-Sanaa's hits is "The Listener's Dedicated Song." The broadcast is meant almost exclusively for the male public but, being presented by a woman, it breaches the hard and fast customs of Islam—for muslim zealots a woman's voice should not be heard lest it inspire lust.

"I dedicate this song 'From him to him' to my dear Ahmed in Ryiad, Saudi Arabia."

Thousands of Yemenites have left to go break their backs labouring for their millionaire neighbor. Thanks to radio, thanks to planes and mail service, homesickness doesn't weigh so heavily today in the hearts of emigrants. In the old days those who left

Yemen often simply vanished, never to be seen again. They would be referred to as ghosts. Any such person would be called "the disappeared one" . . .

Northeast of the city of Saada where land and sky meet, trails of hardened lava stretch out until they melt into the sands. The immense Arrub' Al Khálí desert begins here, covering the entire south of the Arabian Peninsula.

This is where Sheikh Abdallah is sitting in front of his ochre house made with layers of straw, mud and clay. The corners of the flat roof are whitewashed and curve slightly upward; they look like small wings.

The sun beats down.

The Sheikh is motionless in the shade of the wall, surrounded by his bodyguards, his knees pulled up. He has a submachine gun lying across his thighs and a dagger on his stomach; the two weapons form a cross. On the ground in front of him sits a Sony transistor radio.

No one moves. Each is paralyzed under his turban, hanging on to every word of the faraway Arab speaker. Thanks to the absolute silence and the latest in stereos, the voice sounds incredibly close.

The voice finally stops. Sheikh Abdallah gets up and pulls the transistor's strap onto his shoulder. This fine lord doesn't take the time for traditional etiquette and ceremony, he goes straight to the subject. The Sheikh is overwhelmed,

"Wallahi! Did you hear? Sadat visited the Zionist enemy: he took the plane to Jerusalem!"

A radio wave sufficed to propel Sheikh Abdallah from the most ancient past to the most burning issues of the present.

I can't resist.

"What do you think of this trip? Isn't it incredible?"

The man pensively strokes his beard, lifting his eyes to the sky. His guards have their eyes fixed on him.

"May Sadat be blessed if he brings peace. But under one condition, he must not lose honor!"

This is how I learned about one of the greatest acts of our century from a wiseman who looked like a prophet.

Sheikh Abdallah, your cup of tea on November 21, 1977, at the edge of the desert, is one I will never forget.

31

Education and Dreams "On-the-Air"

Since part of the adult population doesn't know how to read yet, new ideas come mainly through radio and T.V. For a long time North and South Yemen, Sanaa and Aden, had a separate and distinct flow of ideas. For a long time the two Yemens fought battles through broadcasts, politically warring through the air waves. Now they have united.

It wasn't until 1975 that television appeared in Sanaa for the very first time, though only in black and white. It was a present from the oil emirates of the Arabian Gulf. These generous donors covered the costs during the first two years. Since then, Sanaa's fledgling T.V. has left the nest. Advertising helps it fly.

In its beginnings the Sanaa transmitter only broadcast a few miles around the radius of the capital. The rest of the country was left to watch Saudi programs. Today, thanks to the powerful relays planted on the peaks of the mountains, Sanaa spreads its ideas and pictures throughout the country.

After a speech by the President of the Republic, a military parade, some political commentary, a religious sermon, a course on

Inspired by Allah, the religious sheikhs are among the stars on Sanaa's TV.

hygiene and a school contest, the happy T.V. viewer enjoys his right to relax, teary-eyed with an Egyptian movie—a catcatenation of sentiment.

Cartoons are of course the children's favorite. And sometimes old people's too. I remember a patriarch with dark elongated eyes like an icon, who was fascinated by the "Adventures of Snow White." He lived them through a T.V. screen placed in front of him on his little prayer rug. Walt Disney dubbed in Arabic made the mouth-piece of his water pipe drop from his mouth.

To each his revolution. T.V. is having its own, exposing Yemenite female faces, unveiled, to millions of Muslim viewers. The anchorwomen of Sanaa are petite and very young, with wide black eyes under a small scarf covering their hair, a last tribute paid to tradition.

Yemenites are crazy about television. T.V. antennas sprout from the most remote villages, the most miserable shacks. In Sanaa's market, women hidden behind the screen of the veil no longer carry the eternal water jug on their heads, instead they carry their brand new purchase: a color T.V. set.

Yesterday's travelers navigated by the stars. Today, on a moonless night through the torrid plain of the Tihama along the Red Sea, all you have to do is set your gaze on the bluish lights which mark off the countryside from village to village. These modern stars shine in the picture boxes set on the beaten earth in front of straw huts. There, entire families seated in a semi-circle in the night's hot humid air, journey from news to dreams.

Stars in the Sky and on the Screen

Not far from the straw hut villages lies the city of Zebid: windowless facades blind to the world, chiseled labyrinth houses baked in the whitewash, mysterious stairways and doors that open onto court-yards winding into more courtyards. Its residents once feared for their safety, but today Zebid is a peaceful city. The ancient wooden gates of its surrounding wall have now been sold to wealthy families, who use them for decoration. Zebid the erudite, once more powerful than Sanaa, seems forgotten in the silence of streets covered with white sand.

Zebid is beyond time.

But it has a movie theatre outdoors, under the stars in the courtyard of a very old house. At the entrance is a poster with the film's title. Next to it some rifles lean against the wall, and on the floor daggers are lined up like a series of commas. A sign says: "The management asks their esteemed guests to please leave their weapons in the coatroom."

The neighborhood doesn't have electricity; the projector operates on a private generator. At night, the alleys to the movie theatre are filled with human fireflies carrying kerosene lamps and electric torches.

Veiled in black, shadows darker than the night furtively enter the little side door reserved for women. One night I climbed the stairway, groping along behind them. I emerged onto a balcony facing the screen. Below us bobbed the men's turbans.

It was a burning hot night. The women took off their veils. I pushed my chair over and sat down next to them. The woman sitting next to me gently took my wrist.

"Who are you? Where are you from?"

I could feel her pulse beating beneath her silver bracelets. O my sister, so close and yet so far!

All major cities in Yemen have movie theatres. With one exception, Saada—but who knows for how long this will be. I remember my visit there. Located in the far north near Saudi Arabia, Saada was still extremely puritanical and far from the devils of progress.

"Here we allow guns everywhere! But not movies! Movies are immoral!"

Mohsen was a tribal man, clad with a submachine gun, rifle, ammunition belt, a large dagger and a knife.

"Weapons are more moral than movies . . ." Mohsen's words may seem strange, but he believed in what he told me. He was sincere. I felt that this warrior was at a bit of a loss. Unconsciously, he could sense his world caving in. Alas, one day he too would be lassoed by Hollywood's Westerns. Already tapes of rock music beat against the surrounding wall of ancient Saada, a city as old as the nearby desert.

Ravenous Consumers of Cassettes

A man is curled up in a tiny closet, a hole which serves as his shop, carved from a wall. The fine-featured patriarch nods his head to the beat, his pyramid of a turban bouncing in time. This Sanaa nylon fabric merchant loves John Travolta.

Yes, the American "Saturday Night Fever" wave has swept as far away as this narrow alley, into the heart of the old city, into Bab-el Yemen the most ancient souk of Sanaa. *Stereo fan lil-alhan*

(The Art of Music Stereo Store) blares its speakers full blast, drowning out the barkers and the cries of second-hand jacket-sellers. Disco pounds against the walls of the towering houses laced with stucco. Over the din you can hardly hear the revving of cars or the putt-putt of Japanese motorcycles. Yemenites play tapes everywhere: at home, driving, taking a walk. Meanwhile, businessmen profit.

One of the walls of the *Stereo fan lil-alhan* is a mosaic of cassettes, the others are decorated with a portrait of a Jersey cow and a view of the Taj Mahal. With his perpetual stream of customers the owner does good business.

"When I opened up in 1974 I was the only one. Today in Sanaa there are lots of shops like mine. At the beginning people were only interested in Yemenite and Arabic music, but soon I had to import rock and disco."

Strangely enough the great woman singer from Egypt, Oum Kalsoum, whose voice brings together the Arab world more than any flag ever will, doesn't seem to please Yemenite ears. Nor does the Lebanese woman singer Fairuz, known as "The Nightingale of the Middle East".

Local music varying little from region to region is still Yemen's favorite. Its shamelessly pirated recordings are enthusiastically received by the public. Sometimes at *Stereo fan lil-alhan* a customer will suddenly jump up.

"It's him! It's Ali! It's Ali on the flute and Ahmed on the drums! See, Ali puts a leather band around his cheeks to hold his breath longer. Fantastic! Ali's such a master!"

Imports of Western music into Yemen are limited mainly to American singers. The others just gather dust. Pat Boone, Tom Jones, Travolta, Donna Summer and the Bee Gees sell like hotcakes. Before reaching Yemen many of these voices traveled through Asia, unscrupulously re-recorded in Singapore.

Indian melodies also have an audience with Yemenites, especially with the many Asians working in Yemen. Yet, it's movies from India which pack the theatres. Like Egyptian films, Indian movies pluck heartstrings but with the addition of superb dances and songs performed in splendid colorful costumes.

Video Craze

The 80's brought the latest toy to Yemen; video.

"I have over a thousand movies!" brags the merchant of Haddad street in Sanaa. Where do you find such variety in Europe or America?

On the wall are Chinese and American posters with a strained king-fu champion grimacing and the sultry smile of Faye Dunaway.

A tornado of dust suddenly stirs up in front of the shop. Brakes screech, a door slams, a peasant jumps out of a Toyota truck. He readjusts his turban, lightly brushes off his skirt, hooks his truck keys to his dagger hilt.

"I want a dozen! It's for a wedding."

Making a racket shooting off old rifles, stuffing yourself and chewing quat are no longer enough for the feast. A real wedding has to show movies.

The merchant explains:

"All this costs a fortune! The peasants are good customers though. They come from far off to stock up on entertainment. In the city, people are satisfied with renting a cassette for two or three days.

"I like Steve McQueen, Bruce Lee, Franco Nero, Roger Moore!" pipes a little voice.

Hussein, not any taller than the counter, is the little gofer boy for the video store. He runs out for coffee and cigarettes and sweeps the floor with a broom twice his size. Hussein also keeps up with video sales in Sanaa and can tell you which ones are in the top ten.

"The ones that really sell are the movies with guns and lots of blood. Musicals are just for women and children. Rockets and space, that's for boys! My brother saw 'Star Wars' ten times."

"We also sell educational films!" corrects the merchant owner, worried about his business seeming too frivolous. "Science and foreign language courses . . ."

How to learn English no doubt passed the test but others don't escape the severe eye of censorship. If the Arabs accuse an author of collaborating with the State of Israel, his works are banned to Yemenite viewers. For years films flirting even remotely with communism were as carefully hidden from the Sanaa audience as were, and still are, movie stars's breasts.

Violence goes unveiled, however. Shooting American-style, impaling Chinese-style, strangling Japanese-style, the bodies collapse, the faces cringe. The audience doubles over laughing.

These movies come from Saudi Arabia, the U.S., London,
Hong Kong and Singapore.

On Sanaa's Stage

Faced with this foreign invasion the Ministry of Information and Culture is trying to keep the soul of Yemen alive. Dances and music which have come down through the ages are now carefully recorded, region by region. They are faithfully taught in spacious halls at the center of Sanaa. Lacking enough dance teachers, the Ministry had to import them from Egypt, Korea and the Soviet Union. What a sight, the high cheek-boned couple from Uzbekistan teaching Yemenites . . . Yemenite dances! And with such talent! Before Sanaa, the Uzbeks went from village to village throughout Yemen, astutely observing musicians and dancers.

Some villages dances are very old. They go back to the times before the strictness of Islam, when boys and girls naturally held hands while dancing. These dances created a scandal when they were performed by the Sanaa troupe—just like the slightly undressed bodies now forbidden in painting exhibits.

One night at a performance, the eye of The Muslim Brothers was watching over men and women dancers who were freely tracing out the forms of ancient figures. At the "obscene-sight of touch" the fanatics' insults began to fly. The performance was halted. Future television broadcasts were cancelled.

For "proper" people in Europe and America at the turn of the century an actor was a good-for-nothing. Worse was said of actresses. Somewhat of the same thing is going on in Yemen today. Already life isn't easy for the male actors of the National Theater. Without the dedication to their work the life of the three young women comedians would be martyrdom. A woman who laughs and cries in public, her face unveiled and naked, how indecent! And what a bizarre idea to have a woman play the role of . . . a woman!

Female comedians are sometimes insulted in the street or even harassed by religious fanatics, more pitiful than faithful.

'You are the fall of Islam! . . .' growls a poorly shaven man, brushing by the ravishing Madiha in the theater courtyard.

Madiha el-Haidary, twenty years old, mother of a ten-month old baby and married to the troupe director Palestinian Hussein el-Asmar, has thrown out the window—and out stage left—tradition and the veil.

"My reputable family rejects me. My aunts are staying away from me. My uncle doesn't want me in his house anymore. My father keeps repeating, 'You've dishonoured us!' Everytime a re-

"She plays like an angel and sings like a nightingale". Playing on her "oud", Nabaat Ahmed is one of the very rare women musicians who perform in public.

Some posters in Hodeyda, a city on the Red Sea. Movie star's nudity is carefully hidden from the Yemenite eyes but violence goes unveiled.

hearsal went past sundown it was a scene at home. One night there was an officials' gala performance which went past ten o'clock. I found the door to the house locked . . . and my suitcase in front of it."

Madiha sighs.

"It's hard for us women. But our passion for drama saves us. One of my girlfriends, crazy about acting, couldn't give it up. Today, persecuted by her family, she performs in hiding . . . veiled."

After all, that's nothing new. In Europe and America the road for women hasn't exactly been lined with daisies. I feel like comforting Madiha, so petite and so brave:

"Around 1900, people gossiped about my grandmother—who wasn't yet the mother of my father. To hell with hat-veils and lace! The daring girl hopped a train to Germany, all alone, without a chaperone. In Berlin she gave up her caged-up life for an artist's life. What a scandal when back home they heard that the pure young girl was drawing nudes at the Academy!"

Madiha bursts into laughter. I've won her over. But my story isn't finished yet.

"My pioneer of a grandmother was also a pianist. But she was a woman. She wasn't admitted into the composition course, 'Women might know how to tickle the ivories but they couldn't create.' "

Women, incapable of creating. Women, not capable of anything. Yesterday in Europe and America, today in Yemen. The litany hasn't changed.

Madiha wears a small piece of gold jewelery around her neck, a miniature Koran suspended on a chain. She quickly unhooks it, offers it to me with a smile. I kiss her soft cheek. We understand each other.

The National Theater's young troupe isn't enchained though. The Ministry of Information and Culture seems to give it free rein and the troupe's program is varied. Not only can the Arabian saga of the golden years of Islam be seen on stage, but also the humourous Bernard Shaw, the political Bertolt Brecht and the surrealistic Slawomir Mrozek.

Painters Who Paint Freely

The most apathetic paper-pusher in Mississippi would look like a social climber next to the nonchalant bureaucrats floating around *40* the Sanaa Ministry of Information and Culture.

Even though bureaucrats are asleep in Yemen, painters are awakening. Figurative, abstract or decidedly surrealistic, their paintings decorate the drab walls of the Ministry. After traditional art, admirable but fixed in time; the ornamentation of facades, the rich colorful mysteries of stained-glass windows, the silver of filigree, the mosaics and arabesques, after calligraphy—here are portraits, landscapes, bursting colors. Here are dreams set free.

Hashem Ali Abdallah is one of the masters of the paintbrush. He lives in Taiz in the warm dusty ambiance of his modest apartment. He shakes his black disheveled mane, obviously an artist. Holding his pencil in one hand and his youngest child with the other, he explains:

"Not a single verse in the Koran literally forbids the drawing of the human face. This idea is simply an interpretation of The Holy Book, an interpretation by religious leaders at the beginning of Islam. They were battling pagan cults, trying to discourage the Prophet's followers from worshipping the images and statues of pagan gods."

Well! There's one myth at last swept away . . . with one stroke of a paintbrush!

Hashem has never left Yemen:

"I was invited to Moscow but I refused. For my first trip I want to go to Paris, or to Italy, birthplace of the Arts."

Hashem the Yemenite, isolated at the furthest tip of Arabia, knows more about art than many spoiled Europeans and Americans with libraries and museums at their disposal. Hashem has seen it all: the virgins of Raphael, the trompe l'oeil of baroque, the foliage of Corot, the women of Renoir, the collages of Braque. Hashem has read every book. Like so many others he's come to the conclusion that Cezanne is the master of modern painting.

"One must never stop experimenting. Every idea is worth a try, even the craziest!"

I interrupt his enthusiasm.

"When I was in New York, I saw an exhibit in a gallery, priced at one thousand dollars: a pile of bath towels knotted with a pink bow and decorated with a shoe. A bit much, don't you think?"

Hashem hardly blinks an eye:

"Why not? Art is polymorphic, this was an experiment like any other."

To think that I thought of myself as avant-garde.

"You say you believe in progress in art. Do you also believe in progress in politics?"

"I'm an artist. I think politicians just waste money. They're like chickens who scratch the earth with their feet, throwing the feed we give them to the wind."

Abdeljabbar Noman, another star in the renaissance of Yemen's painting, paints in pastel colors (yellow, blue, pink) history, folklore, tradition and . . . in a glorious green (the color of hope) scenes of the Revolution. Long live the Republic!

Fuad el-Futaih looks like a sad El Greco. He also has a German wife, two kids and a cat. Fuad captures his dreams in a net of minute lines. His art is a delicate mixture of East and West, of Yemenite folklore and Art Deco. His works (pen and inks, engravings, drawings) have traveled as extensively as he has, in the Middle East, in Europe, in America. Fuad has illustrated a number of books—*and left his mark on this one.*

Fuad el-Futaih won second prize in the contest held in Germany to create a logo for the United Nations' "Year of the Woman".

Women Artists

"Has the 'Year of the Woman' changed anything in Yemen?"

"Not much," answers woman artist Djemila el-Koumayn. "I live a false freedom. My husband understands me but we're surrounded by stagnant air. It suffocates me and the sight of my sisters still imprisoned by tradition, hurts."

Djemila is a feminist at the easel. A warm, direct woman. Her palette's colors are soft, but what strength in her art! In a single line she draws a woman asphyxiated in a bubble, drowning in water.

I recognize this picture of imprisonment, always the same picture done by: June in New York, Alix in Geneva, Semiha in Bagdad, Usha in Bombay. Each one expresses it her own way. A mysterious deep-rooted analogy between artists who will never meet each other . . .

This same feeling is also expressed through the verses of the rare Yemenite women poets.

One afternoon I followed one of my Yemenite women friends through the narrow alleys of Sanaa, to the Women's Union. A simple office where they all took off their veils. That day a very young girl had just been sold in marriage. "The poor thing cried . . . ," her mother lamented.

"Aren't there any women who write about all this?" I say.

"A few. Some do it through poetry. Take Amal el-Shamy for example, she writes, but it's been very difficult for her."

After this visit to the Women's Union, I asked everyone about Amal but couldn't get ahold of any of her writings.

Did Amal el-Shamy really exist?

The night before I left Yemen I returned to the hotel to start packing, exhausted. The man at the front desk discreetly pointed out a black mass hidden behind a pillar.

"Someone's been waiting for you . . ." he said.

After women's sundown curfew? And alone in a hotel?

The mass moved toward me, completely covered in black, her face veiled, no eyes showing. From her robes a hand suddenly emerged, disappearing as quickly as it had come out.

I had no time to realize what was happening, the ghost had already left.

In the middle of the hotel lobby I found myself alone, holding a piece of paper: a poem by Amal el-Shamy.

I came across this lovely drawing during my visit to Fouad el-Foutaih's studio, in Sanaa, and thought it was born out of the artist's imagination . . . then the same image appeared suddenly before my eyes the next day on Djebel Sabr, the mountain above the city of Taiz!

43

Everywhere Woman Is Oppressed

Poem by Amal el-Shamy
(Adaptation Laurence Deonna, translation Corinne Borel)

Everywhere woman is oppressed
In villages she is bought and sold.
She must make babies
work from morning 'till night
labor endlessly
in the fields and at home.

And not a word of thanks, not a single 'thank you'

Wind on the Tihama plain near the Red Sea.

Everywhere woman is oppressed
In large towns or small cities
Everywhere divine law goes unheeded.

Mother in misery, miserable mother,
your wounds buried
in the deepest recesses of your heart
distraught and patient
Eternally patient
before blind tradition.

I know, I know
Patience is a virtue
But what about justice?
Only dreams are allowed.

Long live the woman
wrenched by her will for
a better world

Long live her heart
Long live her eyes
Long live her gaze
set on the horizon of light
where love opens

And long live the man
enamoured with justice
Whose words, gaze and gesture
Never claw a woman.

CHAPTER THREE

Modernity, Yes But With Honor

Amran, with a few thousand inhabitants, lies about 30 miles north of the capital. The mayor has gone on pilgrimage to Mecca. Today the city's peace rests in the hands of his turbaned deputy mayor who administrates sitting on a pink cushion. In front of him at the same height as the cushion is his desk, a wooden table painted in bright red.

Set above, the stained glass window colors the room. The walls are whitewashed, the ceilings low. The old man reads with his eyes glued to the paper, his spectacles slipping down on the tip of his nose. I interrupt him:

"Mister Deputy-Mayor, I'd like to meet the chiefs of the tribes, the Sheikhs."

The deputy of the absent mayor lifts his near-sighted gaze, mutters some formalities and mumbles vague words:

"You want to see the Sheikhs?"

What does this woman journalist want anyway?

I drop the subject. Thinking I'm avoiding politics, I point to the kerosene lamp on the windowsill . . . and replunge into the political:

"No electricity?"

"They've begun the work but we've had fights. The tribes, as a matter of fact. Only a few privileged people have generators of their own."

"According to The Plan, isn't electricity supposed to be put everywhere with running water in all the villages?"

"Well . . . you're right, but . . ."

"Why not use the Army to stop the fighting?"

"We'll call in the Army only if the Chinese building the road to Hajja have problems . . ."

The old man doesn't look happy. I suspect he's thinking, "How can a foreigner—and a woman—understand anything about our ways, our problems?"

Here a man's prestige depends on his tribal affiliations. Without the Sheikhs' support, a Republic bureaucrat's influence is like a feather in the wind. Tribal chiefs are masters on their land. Down with the Republic! When the Sheikhs do tolerate progress, they want to control it according to their whims, their traditions. The majority of Yemen's districts were drawn according to borders set by the tribes.

The Tribal Chiefs' Summit

There is no electricity in Amran, but the Arab word-of-mouth telephone does work.

"A foreign lady's here, she wants to meet the Sheikhs!"

Seized by one of the Deputy mayor's two-minute visitors, the news took off through the alleys. It finally found its way to the house—and ears—of a young tribal chief.

Sheikh Houzam Ben Abdallah el-Zaar ran immediately to the Deputy Mayor's office. He walked up through the dark stairway, bent down at the low door, greeted the bureaucrat, and on the spot invited me to follow him.

"Be welcome! I will take you to my people."

I scurry along with three steps to my guide's one in the muddy alley full of armed men, veiled women, curious children, bald cats, and Japanese mopeds.

The buildings are levels of brick and dry mud, frosted with cream-like stucco. Feeling like I'm walking through a wedding cake, I enter the Sheikh's house. I climb up the winding stairs to the top floor, where the "muffredge" is, the men's reception room. Whitewashed and carved with niches, the room looks like a huge sculpture.

I take off my shoes as is the custom here. My bare feet roll on abandoned cartridges lying on the carpet. Submachine guns and rifles are hooked to or leaned against the wall.

On a white background the men sit close together, thin and small, their eyes black, cheeks ballooned out by a cud of quat. The sun splashes red and blue through the ogival stained glass onto the men's faces, turbans, jackets and skirts.

Upon my host's signal, I seat my femininity on the pillow of honor at the prow of the gathering. I am intimidated. I have

After I sat down on the cushion of honor, my host offers me a decoction made with bark and grains of coffee.

penetrated into the impenetrable, into a ritual which is impossible for a stranger to grasp: swift movements of the head and eyes, barely touched welcome kisses, handshakes where deference is allotted according to age and status. You kiss your mother and father on the knee. The Bedouins blow each other a suggestion of a kiss.

"For us, honor is above all!"

What an entrance! But the young Sheikh Houzam is right. Honor has been forgotten in the West. It has disappeared among the metal, concrete and neon lights. Here, between the desert and the Red Sea, tribal life is still based on it. In Europe and the U.S. old women are mugged. In Yemen, never. One can get much farther with a Yemenite reminding him of his honor than by any legal argument.

Listen to this story.

A group of foreigners without a local guide dared to drive on the rocky roads of the country's far north. Planted right in the middle of the road, with submachine guns unquestionably pointed at them, the tribal men ordered them to stop. The thieves took the car and everything inside it. One of them asked the foreigners to strip off their jackets and hand over their wallets:

"Give us your damn development aid!"

The victims were clever.

"Shame on you men of no faith! The traveling stranger is sacred. Have you lost your honor?"

At the insult the thieves paled and stiffened. The victims were able to recover their possessions, and set back out on the road to Sanaa at the steering wheel of their car.

Life isn't always easy for the foreign companies in Yemen building roads, digging trenches for pipes or putting up electric lines. In the wild north honor doesn't keep some tribes from asking ransom or "protection-money". My host in the men's reception room is pushing it a bit when he declares,

"For us honor is above even money!"

Kalashnikov Submachine Guns and Child Soldiers

"And what about guns?" I ask.

"Guns are like honor. They're more than money."

I haven't exactly stumbled onto a church boys' choir.

There are numerous military check posts across the country. Sometimes along the road at the entrance to towns, silhouettes of

The little boys from the Yemenite tribes dress as warriors. Their daggers join them to the clan of men, to which they will really belong once they have reached the age of fifteen. But Sanaa's regular army presently enlists young men at the age of twelve.

fake wooden soldiers remind you to behave. Carrying firearms has been illegal in big cities since 1974; the authorities bought back thousands of rifles at high prices. But once on tribal territory you're back in the "Wild West" of the North. Only a few dozen miles north of Sanaa stereotypical Yemenites appear: men in turbans with their entire arsenal.

Arms symbolize virility. All are armed from the tribal chief to the most ordinary man. A boy at fifteen is a warrior. Young children are clad with daggers, pistols and even assault rifles bigger than they are. In the market, kindergarten-size camouflage uniforms are piled up on tables for the enjoyment of children and the wallets of merchants. The regular army of the Republic of Yemen hires twelve year old child-soldiers.

The Soviet Kalachnikov machine gun is fashionable in the North. It is openly sold in markets among tomatoes and spices. You can still find a few Mausers and Lee-Enfield antique guns which old men dote over lovingly. Their khol-lined eyes watch tenderly over their weapons. They're as meticulous with them as they are with their red hennaed beards.

My host Sheikh Houzam and his peers belong to the most powerful confederation of tribes in Yemen: the Hachids. Today the Sheikhs are holding a summit. An extended family circle . . . but very private. I have dropped in on them . . . like a hair in their cardamom tea! A woman's strand, no less. And yet the Sheikhs are so patient with my persistent interrogation!

The scent of hot coals begins to waft around us. A young man puts glowing embers into the gigantic five foot high waterpipes. The mouthpieces are passed from one to the other, from mouth to mouth, with long tubes snaking around on the floor. The man on my right, after having wiped off the reed of his pipe on his sleeve, offers it to me. I inhale forcefully. In vain. The Sheikhs are amused by the stranger incapable of making the smallest glub glub.

I let go of the pipe and pick up my camera.

"Could I take a picture of you?"

Their faces cloud over. I sense a lack of enthusiasm. They debate. My host politely pleads my cause and they finally agree, reluctantly. What democrats, I almost expected them to vote!

"What are you going to talk about today?" I persist.

"About our business: marriages, inheritances, tribal boundaries and water distribution. We are peasants and we all own our land."

The man on my left, with a powerful voice—and breath— attempts to whisper a secret to me which everyone hears:

"We also set things straight with other tribes . . ."

"And what about the State?"

"The State has to be very strong to be a referee."

"And the President of the Republic in Sanaa?"

"He's just an official. An official from over there . . ."

The Sheikh points towards Sanaa. The message is clear: "Our tribal paths don't always go through the capital."

But you have to make amends with those on high. Hanging on the wall, between a submachine gun and a Koran in its own silken embroidered bag, the President of the Republic, properly-framed, overlooks the assembly.

Lost in far away Yemen and surrounded by armed men, I talk guns—me the pacifist:

"Did you know that where I'm from, in Switzerland, all men are soldiers and they always keep their guns at home?"

My neighbor is thrilled.

"Us too!"

Enthralled by the similarities between Yemen and this remote European country, he leans toward me,

"The Swiss are right. You have to be on guard, the gun at your fingertips. Danger always lurks here . . . with these people who don't listen to God's words and go by the name of 'democrats" . . ."

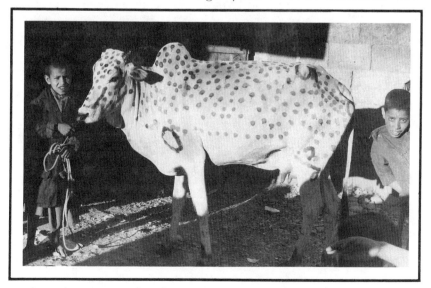

This spotted cow is not of a special breed. It was painted with henna for the *Aid Kebir* (The Sacrifice of Sheep) celebration which takes place two months and ten days after the Ramadan. Pulled by the children, the cow will be walked through the alleys of the village before being slaughtered.

Could I be wrong? I wonder if the "danger that lurks" isn't also a danger of losing power. Dealing with "these democrats" some Sheikhs, even if in Parliament, may feel that they have become just like any ordinary man, an ordinary deputy holding only a few crumbs of power in his hand.

"The Red" and "The Devourer" Sitting in Parliament

A state within the State, the northern tribes' strength goes back in time, rooted in history. Even today, the country's legends are full of their exploits. Since the Revolution their insurrections, squelched either by the regular Army or by money from the Republic, die down only to reemerge later.

My hosts, the Hachids, have the North. The Bakils, the second strongest tribe, have the Northeast. The Zaranigs have the West. The Hamdans populate the villages surrounding Sanaa. Other smaller groups are scattered throughout the country.

Won over by progress and by the lure of quat (I mean a carrot) some tribes close to the cities have sided with the government. In Sanaa I came across a tamed tribal chief.

"Why should I fight the Republic, they made a bureaucrat out of my son!"

The father was radiant beneath his turban at the thought of his bureaucrat-offspring in a three-piece suit.

"I'm proud of him. My son has an education!"

In 1974 President Hamdi, a progressive, made a risky move. He dissolved the Parliament installed by the Revolution. The response was immediate; so were the fights. Essentially, the Assembly was dominated by powerful old-liners, the aristocratic lordly chiefs of the northern tribes. One of them was the great Sinan Abou "el-Loukhoum" ("the Devourer"), chief of the Bakil tribe. The legendary Abdallah "el-Ahmar" ("the Red"), Sheikh of Sheikhs, supreme chief of all Hachid tribes reigned at the head of Parliament.

I'd Rather Have My Sheikh Than the State

"How do you elect your chiefs?"

The fine featured Sheikh Houzam, a man with almost tender eyes, has left the room. He returns offering me a tiny cup, a concoction of coffee bean husks, one of the country's specialties.

He's the one who introduced me to the subtleties of Yemen. He continues,

"Every family chooses its "aakil", a wise man. Among these men every village elects its Sheikh. The Sheikh of Sheikhs is then elected by all the village Sheikhs."

A Sheikh has immense authority. He is the one who exercises justice; in his home, outside under a tree or in the shade of a wall. While awaiting judgement petitioners line up their weapons before the Sheikh's cushion: rifles, submachine guns, daggers are given to him as a security and to show allegiance.

The Sheikh chastizes thieves, reconciles heirs, pacifies neighbors, punishes hit-and-run drivers, decides the distribution of water and writes to the administration. The system is efficient. The dirty laundry is washed among family. The procedure isn't loaded down with paperwork or red tape. Anyway, the interested parties often don't know how to read.

The Sheikh of Sheikhs, the supreme authority, doesn't judge personal matters. He takes care of conflicts between the tribes of his confederation and between his tribes and those outside his territory.

The application of law varies from tribe to tribe. Sometimes tribal law overrides religious or State law. Many Yemenites only recognize their own Sheikh as their judge. To them the Minister of Justice's stationery is just the right size for wiping off their hands. The Republic has thus resigned itself to compromise with tradition and to pay the Sheikhs a salary for their cooperation.

These punctual payments come in addition to the periodic sums received by the Sheikhs for specific services rendered to the State and its people. They play an unofficial role as intermediaries, consultants and accessories to speculation. Many among them are seated in the Parliament.

I remember an old man, standing for hours at the entrance to the Parliament under the gate's arch. He had come from a far away village, dragging a cow as emaciated as he was. He leaned his back against sacks of wheat, left there to be sold to bureaucrats at a reduced price. In one hand he held the animal's rope and with the other he brandished a photo of his son, hit by a car a few days earlier. He had walked a long time to claim justice, carried on two frail legs and a long stick. He cried like a lost child:

"They killed my son! I want to see my Sheikh, not a bureaucrat!"

Crime and Punishment

It's a tragedy to cause a fatal accident in Yemen. For the family of course, but also for the driver, guilty even if the victim threw himself under the wheels. The death of an adult man is expensive, very expensive.

Yemenite justice has softened since the Republic. The hands of thieves are no longer amputated. The death penalty is not always applied for homicide; the victim's family may pardon the guilty party, but generally they demand a large sum of money. That's the State's justice. But for some far away tribes, justice remains what it's been for centuries.

Being a convict in Yemen isn't shameful. In villages you may well run into a person dragging his chains in the marketplace, chatting with passersby. Relatives feed the prisoners. Though always in chains, they are allowed to visit their families from time to time.

I tried to meet the director of a detention jail in Sanaa. I had heard of one who worked in a building of ancient stones, a former palace where greenish water gurgled from an abandoned fountain.

It was noon, prayer time; the stagnant air was suffocating on the deserted street. In vain I knocked at the huge door. I was looking for a soul, any soul who could tell me something about this place. I only found one, it belonged to a prisoner.

"Psst!"

I raised my head. A man had his face glued to the bars, his young eyes sparkling under a saffron turban.

"Are you looking for someone? The prison is closed. They're all at the mosque. Everybody: the director, the guards, the secretary, everybody!"

While those in charge were at prayer, an old man full of nostalgia roamed around the grounds; a former prison guard who had lived the days of the Turkish occupation. Face yellowish and wrinkled, beard dyed flaming red with henna, he hid his eighty-eight years and his nearsightedness behind thick spectacles. He wasn't only looking for old jailkeeper memories though, he was on the lookout for the warden; he wanted to collect his pension.

"When are they coming back?" asked my interpreter.

"Allah only knows . . ."

While waiting, the old man was all too happy to confide to a stranger:

Sanaa. Cadis (Muslim judges) deep in conversation in front of an ancient palace, now transformed into a jail.

Sanaa. A Cadi reads off the judgments he passed that day. His grandson sits next to him.

"Life was good in the time of the Turks. They kept their word. They were generous. When a Turkish officer stopped for coffee in a village, he always gave a silver coin to the person who came to hold his horse."

"And under the Imam?"

With a gesture of disdain the retiree dismissed my question.

"And since the Revolution?"

The same gesture swept away modern times . . .

"Let's go!" said my interpreter dragging me away. "He's babbling."

The Census and Statistics Mystery

Getting back to my story. I am still in Amran spending the afternoon with Sheikh Houzam and the others of the Hachid tribe. I'm still being indiscreet, but still allowed on the pillow of honor.

"How many people are there in your confederation of tribes?"

Silence.

The Sheikhs look at each other nervously. The man sitting next to me finally opens his mouth:

"I don't know. All I know is that our group has five thousand men under arms."

I translate: a tribe's population being calculated by its warriors means that the group has five thousand men over fifteen.

"Only five thousand under arms? You're kidding! Much more!" bleats a one-eyed man. A fight? Trachoma? I'll never know.

I'll never know about the tribes either. Inspired by the Arab "Old Book of Schemes" which makes a virtue of lying, tribes, depending on the moment's strategy, inflate or deflate the numbers of their men. For some, the Hachids represent twenty percent of the population; for others, they are barely ten percent and for still others, they are much less. Not a single stranger, whether he comes from Paris . . . or Sanaa, will ever be able to penetrate the secrets of those rebellious tribes. Rebellious . . . With their lips sealed.

The regular Army, the Army of the Republic, is just as mysterious about its numbers. Secretiveness is a virtue common among Yemenites. A high official of the Sanaa government confided to me,

"Here you hide your age, your religion, and even your politics . . ."

Taking a census of the Yemenite population is a real challenge. Some years ago several organizations trying to take a census in

The new Justice Building in Sanaa, two floored, with half lunettes of stained glass, uniting ancient and modern forms. Similarly, the judges seek to mesh the old with the new, in practise and spirit.

The old-fashioned way (Amran, in the north).

North Yemen found themselves in a desert of imprecision. Their research, based on vague figures (the number of Yemenites who payed the "zakaat", religious tax) and vague replies gleaned here and there through questionnaires, concluded with just as vague statistics: 4 to 9 million people.

In 1975 the United Nations estimated North Yemen's population at 6,480,000. North Yemen was wild, isolated, emptied of a third of its men through emigration and over the years had received thousands of countrymen from the South. Anyone who knew Yemen laughed at this pseudo-exactness. By contrast, the bureaucrats dreaming of a nice tidy Yemen were delighted.

But a Germanic Yemen would have no charm!

In 1975 Swiss experts from the Organization for Technical Cooperation and Census-Taking came to the rescue of Sanaa's authorities. The Swiss invaded Yemen. By Land-Rover they went from mountain peaks to valley floors. By plane they surveyed the country in search of the most remote hamlet, the most godforsaken encampment.

Perfectionists obsessed with precision, the Swiss were the right ones for the enormous job of putting the entire population of North Yemen into a computer without omitting the most mobile emigrant or the most ephemeral nomad. The alleged Yemenites were registered at the place they happened to be—or where they were passing through at the census takers' arrival. Soldiers from the regular Army, on the other hand, were registered with their village or city of origin.

In 1981 the meticulous Europeans were still at it. More free Yemenite butterflies were pinned down by the Swiss.

The Sanaa government backed the census-takers with a publicity campaign. Radio, press and flyers appealed to the population to cooperate. "We have to know how many of you there are to be able to build roads, schools and clinics." For their extensive operation the campaigners even put stickers on packs of cigarettes. Yet it didn't occur to them to use the plastic bags wrapping the bundles of quat . . .

In spite of all this rallying, the Swiss' path was a rocky one. There were stones on the roads, tribal guns pointed at them and many meals too rich but impossible to refuse. Some men hemmed and hawed at revealing the numbers of their women, their daughters and wives.

Guides would suddenly freeze at the edge of a remote canyon.

"Go on alone! This is the end of my tribe's territory. We're on bad terms with the neighbors!"

In the Northeast the census-taker loses his bearings even with a compass. There, a vast land stretches out with uncertain, even nonexistent borders. Where does Yemen end and Saudi Arabia begin? "Yemenites" and "Saudis" are often descendants of the same tribe. For them Sanaa or Riyadh, Yemen or Saudi Arabia, what difference does it make? Without any qualms "Yemenites" forget their "nationality" at the doors of the Saudian Emir of Najran's free modern clinic. Najran is a hilly territory tufted with palm groves laying between Djebel Razih and the Katif province.

For years at the south of the map, the line between the two Yemens was drawn according to political trends. In 1990 the Republic of Yemen was born. Borders were retraced outlining a Yemen which had never before existed in history. Today's storytellers are already creating legends of the new power at the tip of the Arabian Peninsula: 12 million Yemenites with approximately 9.5 million from the North and 2.5 million from the South. This new neighbor may not be altogether palatable to Saudi Arabia's 7 million. . . .

One Fine Night in Saada

For my journey to the far north of the country I found the perfect guide. A stranger to the north, his good reputation spread beyond the borders of his tribe. He's a peasant-cum-cassette vendor, a pioneer of the Koran-on-tape. The muezzin's song is his gold mine, an eternal hit . . .

He's wearing a white turban, an almond-green robe and a violet coat. His large dagger slid into a silver sheath is held by a wide belt embroidered with arabesques.

Matari is his name. He has a thick mustache, pointed black Assyrian beard and a hearty Homeric laugh. Like Mata-Hari the famous French spy, he likes dancing, but warrior dancing to the beat of a drum among a circle of men brandishing arms.

"So are you interested in state secrets like Mata-Hari?"

Matari bellows with laughter.

"Not as much as the secrets of beautiful poetry."

"Do you know a poet here in Saada?"

"Poets are everywhere in Yemen! One of them lives very close by, a friend. We'll stay at his house."

Saada is surrounded by the protection of an enormous mud wall. To enter the city we pass underneath the arch of its huge   63 gates. Darkness is upon us. Nights in the lower Orient fall suddenly. The slow veiling of colors of our northern sunsets is unknown here.

Lifting your head up in Saada is to behold a fairytale; the silhouettes of roofs are a white lace against the starry sky. Lowering your head is to imagine yourself caught in a death-trap, robbed, raped, never to be seen or heard from again. But in reality what nice people. With a kerosene lamp in his hand, one of the few passersby offers to guide us through the maze of alleys. Matari follows the dancing light before him. I walk at his heels.

Behind the low doorway of a high mud house we hear the news.

"The poet's in prison."

"In prison? Why? A brawl?" I ask.

"Something to do with money."

Matari isn't surprised.

"Let's go say good-night to him."

The prisoner-poet greets us by the light of the moon, behind the bars of his temporary home. He laughs and exchanges whispered words with Matari, who pretends to fill me in.

"Nothing serious."

I'll never know more.

A passerby informs me that people in Saada can have problems with the police if they have strangers in their house overnight. The police may just be taking precautionary measures, though. The city is near Saudi Arabia, in the middle of the agitated north where some rebellious northern Yemenite tribes have close links with their powerful neighbor.

We still have to find lodging. The hostel is overcrowded . . . and I'm a woman! In this caravanserai you only snore among men, twenty to a room on iron beds with broken boxsprings and mattresses too thin. The powder room is powdered with dust and the bucket of water there isn't enough to wash away the stream.

Finally, Matari brings me to sleep at the school where I make myself comfortable on the wooden floor. He then disappears to God knows where. I won't see him until morning.

Hello, Hello!

At nine o'clock the next morning I pay a visit to the Mayor-Governor of Saada, an unturbaned man with a long face, wearing a tight western-style jacket and pants. A white telephone is displayed on his table. Facing him, sitting down on the ground, threaded along the wall, dozens of visitors are lined up clad in their arsenal, legs folded and patient.

The magistrate lightly taps on his telephone, puts his ear to the receiver and sets it back down, turning to me:

"I have a dial tone, everything works! My phone is connected through the Army's radio."

Since 1981 telephone connects Sanaa, the capital, to the provinces. But earlier at the time of my visit to Saada, it wasn't yet the case. In those pioneering days everything was still a bit haywire. Telephone surrealism had caught-on in Yemen. An incomprehensible language spoken on a recorded message informed the Yemenites, "This number has been disconnected." Sometimes it added, "Please consult your new phone book." One of the companies which installed phones in Yemen was French. So was the mysterious voice. There was no telephone book in Yemen.

No Hold-up

Buckling under the weight of a burlap sack marked "Minneapolis USA," a man pushes through the door of the office with his shoulder, sets down his load, digs through his pocket and hands the magistrate a piece of paper. My host reads it and signs.

"What does this sack of wheat have in it?" I ask.

"Money. Banknotes. The bureaucrats' payroll," the Governor replies.

The golden "sack of wheat" is carried like this, without escort, through

A standing telephone is a must for the Yemenite who wants to be well seated in society. The center of the dial-plate is sometimes used as a frame for the photograph of one of the family's sons.

a building full of armed men! I'm impressed.

No hold-ups at the outdoor money changers' either. Their roof is a beach umbrella, their counter a wax tablecloth laid on the beaten earth where they pile up the bills. Every day thousands of Yemenite and Saudi rials go through their hands. And within reach of everyone. But no one touches it. These outdoor bankers are also arms dealers in the open.

Matari runs into a friend in front of the mosque. He's Ibrahim, forty years old with two intense eyes, three gold teeth and an apple-green jacket and turban. His resplendent colors and air of nonchalance are so far from the grey hurried forms of the West.

In his large belt, behind his "jambia", Ibrahim has slid in a knife, a pair of scissors, a notebook, a pen, a pair of glasses, a small hard brush and toothpicks. Truck keys jingle on his dagger's handle.

"Yes, I travel light! My belt is my suitcase!" he says.

Ibrahim does business.

"What kind of business?"

"All kinds of business!"

A Marketplace Unlike Others

Twelve miles from Saada, and thirty-five from the Saudi border, a village sits out in the desert: souk El-Talh. This market was created during the Revolution to allow business to go on in peace, far from the city's bombings. Today it sells everything which goes legally or illegally through Saudi Arabia, the immense next-door-neighbor.

On the first day of the muslim week, from Friday night to Saturday night, millions of rials change hands in souk El-Talh without the Yemenite government being able to collect a single rial of tax.

The bazaar merchants keep shop sitting in dry mud cubicles; others sell directly from their trucks, cases of smuggled stereo hi-fi's, cigarettes, cans, fabrics and so on.

Souk El-Talh is the desert's permanent auto show. Mazdas and four-wheel-drive Toyotas are the most popular. A Mazda costs five times more in Sanaa than here. The long trip to the desert souk is well worth it. Even for a buyer from the capital who will later have to pay for license plates and customs fees, it's still a good deal.

If the buyer lives in the north he doesn't bother to pay customs fees and drives without plates. The governor of Saada attempted to bar these cars from entering the city. In vain. In Saada, one can drive in a new unplated car with no identification except for the importer's sticker on the windshield—importers from Djeddah on the Red Sea, Kuwait or any other port on the Arabian Gulf.

In the war department of souk El-Talh bazookas, pistols, grenades, Czechoslovakian revolvers, old 1943 French rifles and English ammunition still wrapped in packages, surround the king of guns, the Yemenites' dearest: the chromed Kalachnikov submachine gun.

Not only do civilians enjoy this arsenal, but the police are also good customers. In 1981 the Yemenite State allegedly forbid the conspicuous sale of weapons and began collecting a customs tax on arms displayed at souk El-Talh. Mouths are sealed as to exactly how the arms have gotten here, but they do open up a little bit about their origins: Syria, Lebanon . . . yet, it's impossible to find out. Thousands of trucks go back and forth between Mediterranean harbors and the deserts of Arabia. The Saudis don't seem to interfere, though the guns used by the Mecca insurgents in 1979 may well have been purchased in this faraway place.

Whiskey is the only thing missing at souk El-Talh. It crosses the arms route from the opposite direction, discreetly going from a Yemenite harbor to the hideaways of Saudi Arabia.

Maria-Theresa Always Popular in Spite of Paper Money

At the souk El-Tahl, thalers are piled up into small pillars in front of the money changers, sitting on the ground. Minted since 1780—and always imprinted with this same date—the Maria Theresa thaler is a heavy silver coin which Yemenites insist on calling "the French rial". Until the fall of the Yemenite monarchy, the thaler, along with bartering, was the only form of exchange. The thaler also circulated in East Africa, Ethiopia, on the coast of the Red Sea and in the Arabian Peninsula's south. Throughout the region the coin more or less played the role of a standard currency, just as the sterling pound, and later, the dollar did in the rest of the world.

Navigators and merchants chose the thaler not for historical, political or monetary reasons but for its high silver content. Until World War I, Austria was the only country authorized to mint it. England, Italy, and Belgium later joined in. In 1963 Austria re-established its exclusive rights. Today the new thalers are only made for numismatists.

Since the Revolution, thousands and thousands of effigies of this empress, as far away in time as in space, have been melted down in Yemen for new uses. Today people want gold. But the silver profile of Maria-Theresa of Austria and her abundant breasts can still be seen hanging on the heavy pendulous necklaces, adorning the more modest chests of many Yemenite women. Jewelry is capital for peasant women, they wear their "savings account" around their neck. It's also said that some tribes of the earth and sand consider paper money worthless and still prefer the sound of a good silver thaler.

The civil war slowed Yemen's attempts at creating a modern monetary system. The first paper money wasn't issued until 1964, and only in small bills. The largest one, 100 *rials,* wasn't printed for another ten years. Hence the mountains of bills piled up on counters and the size of the safe-boxes, enormous cookie tins anchored with heavy locks.

Though adorned with her impressive thalers necklace, the peasant woman isn't queen of the El-Talh souk. Women discreetly maintain their distance from the men's six-wheel trucks and six-shot rifles. In the shade of a hundred year old tree, the only tree for miles, they sell multicolored baskets, the same sort their ancestors wove thousands of years ago.

I approach a group of these basket sellers comfortably seated on their heels and squat down near them. Now we are at the same level. I sense they're staring me down through their black veils. Then their hands, impatient and probing, feel my clothes, going down my legs; the women are fascinated by my transparent nylon stockings. They giggle and call their friends over. I hope that someday the pioneer of "Pretty Legs" will move his inventory all the way out to Yemen's desert for the pleasure of these women condemned to the past. The men, they already have everything they want.

Matari had tactfully left me alone with the women. Followed by his friend Ibrahim he suddenly reappeared from behind some smuggled Japanese cars. We get back into our own car and once more find ourselves on the pock-marked desert trail.

Dust flies around us. We drive toward Saada. Far off in the landscape I see the outlines of low squat white domes, some large, some small. Ibrahim points them out.

"They're mausoleums, tombs of our cultivated Imams! Yemenites have a civilization! You know what a Saudi once asked me: 'Aren't the presidents of your large companies buried in the big tombs and the vice-presidents in the little ones?' The Saudis are just ignorant bedouins without a history, only good for money!"

True or false, the story speaks for itself. Why deny yourself the pleasure of a light swat at your neighbor who perhaps lacks in civilization but has plenty of oil?

I spent a second night at Saada, once again stretched out on the school room floor, lulled to sleep by the lament of whining stray dogs. The members of this canine choir have short cropped yellow or black fur. They sleep during the day and at night, between songs, take care of the garbage.

Tradition and Revolution

In the morning, I hear Matari's song at my window. He calls me; we're leaving for Khamer.

Lying between Sanaa, the capital of the State and Saada in the far north, Khamer is the capital of the Hachid tribes. The supreme Sheikh Ahmar, the old fox of politics, isn't home. For the time being he resides in his Sanaa palace. I want to at least meet the second-in-command of the Hachids, the young Sheikh Moujahid Abou El-Shawarib who will someday succeed him—if Allah and the tribes will it, of course.

The road travels through an ochre-earth landscape with volcanic rocks and rust-colored stones used to build the city of Khamer. From a distance its walls blend with the horizon. In the scorching light of the sun, its windows stare at you like startled eyes made-up in white. As we approach, the towering fortified buildings begin to stand out more distinctly, imposing against a pure blue sky.

We arrive at high noon. The only sounds heard in the deserted streets are the rumbling of our motor and the barking of dogs. A short-skirted warrior appears in the sun-drenched street. Matari asks for directions. The man looks at us suspiciously. To see the great Moujahid you have to appear as innocent as a lamb. Matari talks, waving his hands, and ends up convincing him of my pure intentions. The warrior walks away, comes back a few minutes later. A smile lights up his weathered features.

"Follow me!"

He walks in front of us all the way to the house. A handsome young man, one of the Sheikh's deputies, invites us into the coolness of a modern "muffredge", a large living room with high ceilings. Once more my female toes fidget on a strictly male treaded carpet— a royal red carpet. Above my head a fake crystal chandelier tinkles.

What luck! Sheikh Moujahid Abou "El-Shawarib" ("The Mustached One") is home today. The men of the tribe await their chief on narrow thin mattresses, their elbows propped up on colorful irridescent pillows. To make room for me, one of them moves his ammunition belt—at "The Mustached One's" you don't have to leave your arsenal at the door.

With an air of nonchalance, I look over the niches decorated with plastic roses and rubber duckies. What children these warriors are! A display of portraits brings me back to more serious things. The father and grandfather of the Master of the house stare fixedly from their picture frame, beards stiff, eyes fierce. Futile to look for a woman in this array of ancestors . . .

Further down the wall I see quotations from the Koran written in golden letters on a black background. Allah's words are zealously applied to every act of daily living.

My imagination wanders; what does Moujahid look like? A peaceful picture from an ancient tale or a modern lean wolf with a cruel eye?

The deputy informs me,

"Our Master is busy but he won't be long. What would you like to know? I will relay the message to him."

The young man picks up a paper and pencil and while he writes my questions down, Matari whispers to me:

"Moujahid didn't go past elementary school. Ahmar, the Sheikh of Sheikhs, didn't go to school at all, he taught himself."

The secretary-deputy lifts his head.

"At fifteen our Master Moujahid entered the school of life, he was already into politics! He spread propaganda against the King. The Bakils backed the Imam, but not us! Not the Hachids! Moujahid fought for the Revolution like a lion. He was put into prison twice as chief of our tribal army. His father and brother were executed by the King."

The deputy insists,

"We wanted nothing else but freedom! For a while we worried whether modernism would lead us astray, but we were wrong, praise be to God. We just want roads, schools and hospitals. Moujahid is Governor, the link between Sanaa and the Hachid tribes. He's strong, he works with his hands. He's generous."

The enthusiastic eulogy continues:

My host, Sheik Moujahid Abou El-Shawarib, chief of the Hachid tribes.

"Our Master is a just and honorable man. He supervises all the development centers on our tribal territory. It's a lot of work because they're spread out and sometimes difficult to get to. Moujahid is also our tribal judge. He resolves disputes between farmers and their landowners."

Lordly Hospitality

A group of men immersed in conversation appear in the doorway. No need to tell me. "The Shawarib" ("The Mustached One") looks just like the other mustached men around him, same clothes, same dagger, same everything; yet from the way he acts, the way he walks, the way he holds his head, you can sense an authority which distinguishes him at first glance.

Market place in Amran.

The Sheikh looks around the room, discovers me between two turbans and approaches. What a piercing gaze! The Shawarib reminds me of the pictures I've seen of Moustafa Kemal, the late Turkish dictator; the same light-colored eyes, the same acuity. My host's eyes have yellow glints like a tiger.

"Please be welcome!"

Sheikh Moujahid bends down to shake my hand.

"Follow me, Madame, lunch is ready."

To go through the corridors with stone floors I have to put my shoes back on. While hopping on one foot, two photos stuck on the wall suddenly catch my eye. On them are Moujahid shaking hands with Mao Tse-tung and Chou En-lai.

The Sheikh has followed my gaze.

"I've traveled a lot. Not only in China but also the Soviet Union."

"What was your impression of Mao and Chou?"

"Mao was a man of theoretical ideas while Chou was more pragmatic."

Did my host, though a fervent traditionalist, have leftist leanings or was this only a subtle political arabesque?

We cross an anteroom. At the dining room entrance two little boys as meticulous as racoons washing their food at a river, pour water over our hands and give us soap and a towel. Again I take off my shoes and we sit, not at the table, but "at the mat".

The food is spread out on a long woven straw mat. What a feast! In this culinary paradise one doesn't pull out the pocket calculator to add up the calories. Yemenites are naturally small and lean.

Moujahid designates a pillow on his left for me. I sit down. The menu is sumptuous: roast lamb, grilled chicken, saffron rice, salads seasoned with mint, fruits and cakes.

"This isn't only Yemenite food, I also like the Arabian Gulf specialties," says the Sheikh.

Here you eat with your fingers, intently, without talking. The bread is pita but almost transparent. It is big and round; you put your food on it and fold it over like a handkerchief.

When the Master of the house is home, meals are open to even the poorest of the tribe. How far we are from the Western segregation of official banquets, where the alleged elite line up their bloated red faces in the thickness of laughter and the reek of alcohol.

Completely attentive to his guests, Sheikh Moujahid hasn't even had a bite for himself yet. Traditionally, he should eat last, after having served all his guests by his own hand.

"Look! Here comes my little youngest."

The chief of the tribe tenderly welcomes the little boy who makes his entrance carrying his schoolbag. The child shyly fidgets, refusing to say hello to the big people. He starts playing with his father's dagger then nestles under his daddy's arm.

The strong black-bearded Sheikh melts, his host-smile softens. The chief of the tribe is transformed into an adoring father. Touched, the warrior is touching; moved, the man is moving. Sheikh Moujahid has become alluring.

Once the meal is finished the guests return to the "muffredge" and get ready for the "quat party". The Sheikh after having played his role as Master of the house, takes his place near the window as Master of the tribe.

I sit near him.

"Sheikh Moujahid you have so much to do!"

"It's my duty. I only do what I am supposed to. The government knows it can count on me to resolve certain kinds of problems."

"How do you see the future of Yemen?"

"I want my country to modernize, but without betraying its traditions. Above all, I don't want it to lose its sense of honor."

"Isn't that asking for the impossible?"

Silence is the Sheikh's reply. I am not surprised. Caught between tradition and modernization, between the Koranic challenge and the American challenge, the Yemenite intelligentsia is still looking for—and perhaps will be for a long time—the path to its evolution.

The Daughter of the Sheikh

I dare a loaded question:

"What do you think of women journalists?"

Taken by surprise, slightly irritated, Moujahid strokes the black curl above his ear.

"Uhh . . . what can I say? I don't know . . . you are the first one to come here."

Being a diplomat and a politician, he hurries to correct himself,

"I don't have anything against it. Women also have a right to education."

Reassured by his reply I ask,

"Do women also have a right to freedom?"

"Why not, as long as they maintain their honor!"

Such well recited lines! O Honor, how many women are kept prisoner in your name!

"And what would you do if your daughter fell in love with a foreigner?"

"She could marry him if he were a man of honor."

It's Shakespeare speaking through the mouth of the Sheikh— and with such noble open-mindedness. Moujahid is avant-garde.

A venerable old man sitting near us tears the reed of his water pipe out of his mouth. The white turban set on his head like a small hatbox indicates he is a cadi, a muslim judge. He's scandalized. In a quivering voice he says,

"Never, never! The Koran says that a woman has to submit. The Koran says: 'A woman has to accept the husband which her father chooses.'"

Under the high turbans agitation is at its peak. My conversation with the Sheikh has fired them up. The chewing smokers only want one thing: to see this bothersome woman journalist kicked out. They want to go back to their obsession; flying away on their beloved drug.

Moujahid doesn't try to keep me. He smiles vaguely as if to say, "You have to take them as they come . . ." And maybe to himself he's saying, "What else could I do but take her as she was . . ." I thank him. For the last time my eyes meet his striking yellow gaze.

Matari reluctantly gets up from his cushion, leaving behind his pipe and the room's scented haze. The heavy door closes behind the guide and his bothersome female-traveler-disrupter-of-fine-afternoons.

One block away sits the house of old Ahmar, the supreme chief of the Hachids. Cannons guard his famous home. Matari is surprised by my surprise.

"I know a Sheikh who even hoisted a cannon all the way to his roof! Another salvaged an Egyptian tank after the civil war."

The big Sheikhs are protected night and day by praetorian guards—just like the ancient Romans. Their men are devoted to them body and soul. They can raise an army with the wink of an eye. In Sanaa, seen from the outside, Sheikh Moujahid's city home resembles a medieval fortress. A small door is cut from the huge wooden gate just big enough for a person to enter the inner courtyard. Outside the gate, guards sit in the dust against the wall, permanently on the lookout.

Those Who Didn't Take the Flying Carpets

Matari my guide has to go back to Sanaa on some kind of mysterious business. We have to leave the north and go back to the capital immediately. While we drive, the king of Koran-on-tape plays a cassette. With one hand Matari holds the steering wheel—wrapped in pink plastic decorated in pink roses—and with the other hand, he drums out the song's beat on his thigh.

The road is wide and smooth, the sun isn't scorching yet. We drive through Raida, forty miles from Sanaa.

All of a sudden I see a man wandering along the road, bent under a heavy bundle, shoulder without a gun, belt without a dagger, a skullcap on his head and a face framed by two long curls.

We've come across one of the last Jews in Yemen. Matari slows the car. I want to speak to the man and take a picture of him. He's a woodworker.

The screech of brakes makes me jump. A truck has appeared, overloaded with armed, dusty tribe men. One of the en-turbanned men laughs and points his finger to the wanderer, who hesitates beneath his skullcap. The man yells,

"Moshe Dayan! Moshe Dayan!"

The joker covers one of his eyes with his hand. The imitation of the famous Israeli general makes the passengers piled up on the truck burst out laughing. The truck shakes too.

The "Wandering Jew" pales.

"Don't know anything about Israel! Israel isn't my country!" He insists,

"Yemen is my country. I'm a Yemenite!"

A few days earlier in Saada, a leatherworker who made rough-cut goatskin waterbags and sheepskin cradles, introduced himself to me:

"I am of the tribe of Israel, but I'm a Yemenite. I practice my religion, close my shop on Saturdays. The Sheikhs treat me well, the State leaves me alone. I own two houses."

"Why didn't you take the planes sent by the State of Israel to Yemenite Jews?"

"The planes were leaving from Aden at the other side of the country. The mountains were too high to cross, the road too rocky, the trip too long. When I finally decided to go it was too late, the flights had stopped. There were political problems there also."

"Any news from those who left?"

"Not a thing, ever."

"Can I take a picture of you?"

The biblical Jew's face closed up. Sitting among his skins, knives, threads and scissors, he answered,

"No thank you."

"Why not?"

"It's better that way."

In 1950 the Israeli "flying carpets" brought 50,000 Yemenite Jews from the Middle Ages to a completely modern state. Today, a few thousand remain according to some, a few hundred are left according to others. Some are in Raida but most are in Saada and its neighboring villages. There are none left in Sanaa.

Shoulder without a gun, belt without a dagger, face framed by two long curls, here is one of the last Jews in Yemen. A woodworker, he lives in the north of the country.

In the North, Jewish homes blend in with Muslim homes, nothing distinguishes one house from the other. In their daily life Jews live much like Muslims. When the few Jews who can afford it ride on a Suzuki or a Honda, they look just like Mister Anybody, except for their sidelocks flapping in the wind. Some dare to carry the "jambia" dagger which is theoretically forbidden to Jews, as are all weapons. Others farm a small plot of land, though this is also against practice. Unlike Muslim tradition, Jewish tradition allows the distillation of alcohol. Yemenite Jews use this allowance.

Jewish women, like Muslim women, usually close their doors in the face of a man who is a stranger to the family. Yet in marriage ceremonies, they aren't separated from the men, as is Muslim practice. My guide claims that he's never heard of a mixed marriage between the two communities.

Until the complete exodus in 1950 the Jews of Sanaa lived in their own neighborhood surrounded by a wall. Its gates were closed at sundown like the gates of the muslim neighborhood. While Muslims could build skyscrapers, Jews were only authorized a maximum of two stories.

Jews were artisans. They gave Yemen its enchanting stained-glass windows, delicately worked ornaments and unique silver jewelry. Since they've left silver is no longer crafted as it was. Yemenite women sell their antique silver necklaces, bracelets and rings. Today they want gold, worth its weight.

One morning in Sanaa, in the ancient Bab el-Yemen souk, I was trying on an old silver necklace, a finely worked choker. Suddenly, a voice laughing behind a thick colored veil, called out to me,

"What's a young woman like you doing with this old silver junk! I'm a grandmother and I look for modern gold jewelery!"

The Jews left Yemen though they were well liked. The common Yemenite people didn't really understand the reason for their sudden departure. Were the Jews seduced by the enigma of modern "flying carpets" or was it simply the propagandistic promises, the millenia-old chorus, the return to Jerusalem?

Water, A Precious Gift

And so from tribe to tribe, from Sheikh to Sheikh, I discovered each day a little bit more about Yemen, about its minorities, its customs and habits.

At the end of my provincial tour I found myself back in Sanaa. Once again a Sheikh awaited me, the father of young Sheikh Houzam el-Zaar of Amram. Not only was he a noble patriarch, but he was also an exquisite host. He showed me his house, introduced me to his family. Then suddenly he left and reappeared, carrying cool fresh water in a medieval silver chalice.

The moisture clinging to the metal tempted me. I was very thirsty. But like all Westerners in far away countries I was afraid of water, I hesitated. My guide whispered in my ear:

"Drink! Drink! His offering is a sign of friendship. Once water was so rare . . . You'd offend him if you refused."

Wadir-Dar, not far from Sanaa, was one of the king's palaces; a fortress perched on a rock—and beautified with stucco lace.

Quaintly decorated wooden shutter in Bab-el-Yemen, Sanaa's oldest souk.

In Taiz city, the former king's palace is flanked with multicolored moucharabiehs* in typical Yemenite style. (See glossary)

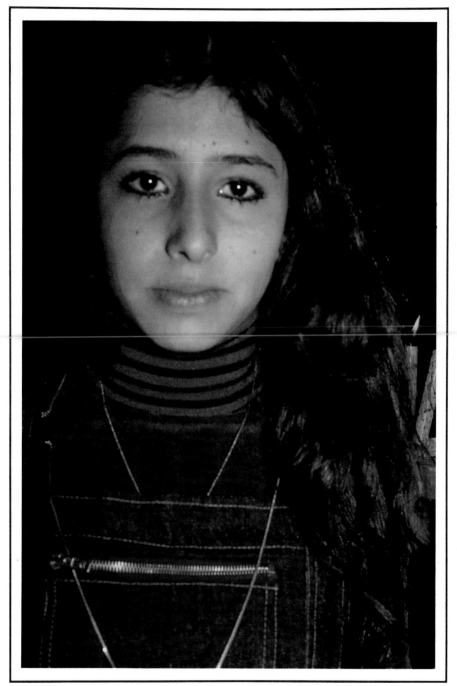

A rare girl. Seventeen year old student Najjat Boulboul didn't wear the veil. Not even a scarf to cover her hair! She hadn't married. Her dream was to publish a feminist magazine in Sanaa.

Street in Bab-El-Yemen souk, the oldest market place in Sanaa.

In souk El Talh, a market on the desert's edge, close to the Saudi border, the merchants sit in tiny dry mud cubicles:

—selling silver— sheaths, bracelets, coins.

—changing Yemenite and Saudi bills.

An old mosque in Zebid, a city near the Red Sea. Story has it that the principles of algebra were discovered here.

An unveiled beauty near Zebid.

Djibla. A mosque "dating from the time of the Prophet" . . .

A minaret in Djibla.

In Djibla, one of the ancient capitals of the land, lived Arwa, a queen as prestigious as the Queen of Sheba.

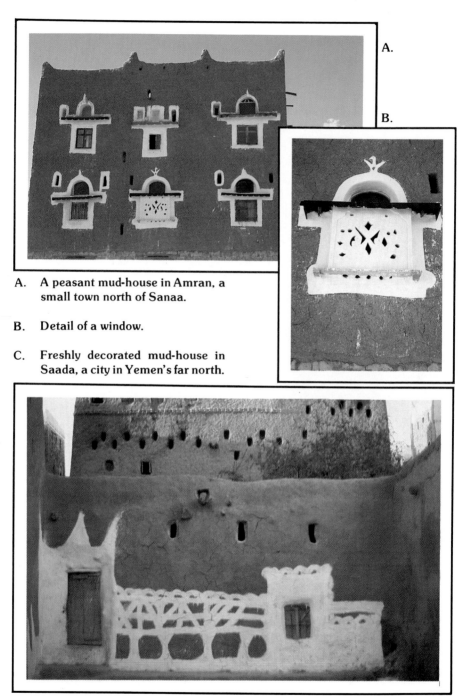

A. A peasant mud-house in Amran, a small town north of Sanaa.

B. Detail of a window.

C. Freshly decorated mud-house in Saada, a city in Yemen's far north.

A rich merchant's palace in Sanaa.

On the Tihama plain, women gather around the well.

These semi-nomadic women belong to Yemen's lowest caste, the Khadams.

On the Tihama plain, along the Red Sea. The little girl wears her "Sunday best", a nylon fabric dress "made in China", but her headdress is typically Yemenite.

Silver craftsmanship made Yemen's name for centuries.

Landscape on the road to Saada, in the north.

The men's reception rooms, embellished with stained glass windows, are located at the very top of houses and enjoy a panoramic view of the city or village.

In the far north, near the Saudi border, a
are sold openly at the El-Talh souk.

The Bab-El-Yemen spice-market, in Sanaa.

Amran. Chiefs of the Hashid tribes holding a summit in Sheikh El-Zaar's
exclusively male reception room.

...ht, public scribe in front of the mosque in ...ration Square, in Sanaa. The man ...ws the Islamic law and is something like ...wyer.

The Bab-El-Yemen souk, in Sanaa. Curled up in his tiny shop, the nylon fabric merchant chews quat. The fabrics are sold for feminine attire.

A rare photograph: women's quarters are not only forbidden to men but also to the camera.

Man reading the Koran.

A.

A. Selling melons on the road between Sanaa and Hodeyda. I thought I managed to catch this—forbidden—snapshot of the woman on the sly, but I was wrong. "I double up the price of your melon", she said, "you've to pay for your sin. And don't try to cheat me or my husband will come and beat you up!"

B. Sanaa. Old woman waiting in front of the mosque in Liberation Square.

C. Women—seen from the back—shopping at the Bab-El-Yemen market. They are dressed after the Sanaa style, wrapped in a large piece of material imported from Pakistan.

D. Women bake the bread at home, then pile it up on a tray which they carry on their heads and — as here in Sanaa—sell it on the streets.

B.

C.

D.

Saada, a city in the far north.

View from the road to Ibb, a small city between Sanaa and Taiz. In central Yemen, villages stand at dizzying heights.

Excerpts from the Yemenite National Anthem (1990) created from the poem by Abdullah Abdel Wahab Noman

O my land
Your sons and grandsons will protect
what you have placed in their hands
This heritage rising out of a great past
will perpetually bathe in light
your rocky slopes,
every grain of your many sands.

O my flag
sewn of suns,
never stop waving at the peaks of our mountains.

I have traveled loving the world
I have followed the Arab path
But the beat of my heart
will always be Yemenite.

CHAPTER FOUR

Quat Going Cheek to Cheek— Money Going Hand to Hand

Every day created by Allah a balloon grows inside Yemenites' cheeks, beginning in the early afternoon and ending when the sun goes down. Except for celebrations, when it puffs up well into the night.

Don't get me wrong, Yemenites don't have chronic toothaches. They chew. They chew quat. The Yemenite who lovingly clutches a green bouquet wrapped in plastic under his arm isn't hurrying to a lover's rendez-vous. He's hurrying to his daily, traditional, ever-so-sacred "quat party."

Describing Yemen without speaking of quat would be like speaking of France's Burgundy region without mentioning wine. For centuries Yemenites have been consuming this luscious plant, grown year round in shrubs on mountain slopes. Its soft oval leaves help one to forget a life which is at best monotonous, at worst miserable. But it also makes your eyes pop out and your spit turn green.

Quat is essential for the Yemenite who wants to "take a trip" or offer one to his friends or guests. Not a single birth, not a single marriage, not a single business or political meeting takes place without Yemenites all chewing in harmony.

They skillfully pull the leaves off twigs and pinch off the tenderest shoots. They then chomp up the leaves and roll them into a little ball tucked between the cheek and teeth. All around the chewers the ground becomes covered with a dusty carpet of leaves. *105*

Sitting all together in a warm, soft light, Yemenites slowly slide into bliss. Worries vanish, minds sharpen, ideas flourish, inspiration is born. Poems blossom, ancient verses long forgotten are brought back to mind.

To perfect the high, some gluttons take everything at the same time: the cud of quat, the cigarette, the water pipe and sometimes even . . . a drop of whiskey.

At the center of the room big-bellied barrels made of red and white plastic have replaced the old-time earthenware water jugs. They are thermoses "Made in China," holding the cool fresh water used to rinse out the mouth.

"I like progress," gurgles an old man with bare gums. "I'm a widower to all my teeth but I can grind up my quat with my new deluxe coffee grinder. Everyone is jealous of my quat balls."

For many Yemenites, quat, a stimulant and euphoric, is the universal remedy, soothing toothaches and torments of the soul. It's a veritable panacea.

Says: a taxi-driver, "Thanks to quat I can drive for hours without getting tired!"

a student, "Thanks to quat I can tell my father that I flunked my exams!"

a journalist, "Thanks to quat I can write my article in one sitting!"

a first wife, "Thanks to quat I can stand the idea of a second wife!"

Quat is a false friend, though, It has properties resembling cocaine and opium and its effects are like those of amphetamines. Regular consumption can lead to serious complications. The quat addict has a dry mouth, abnormally dilated pupils, frequent urinary retention and constipation. His appetite diminishes, then eventually disappears. Minor gastric problems become chronic. His nerves become on edge and his undernourished body loses resistance to disease. He doesn't sleep anymore. His sex-drive goes down. He may fall into a depression. Chewing the quat balls may injure his mouth's mucous membranes, which then harden. The unrepentant quat addict increases his risk of cheek cancer.

Satan at Your Mouth

Quat is chewed from puberty on. I remember a fifteen year-old boy with hollow eyes, a washed out face and a distended belly. He was lying on a bed in a Kuwaitian hospital in Sanaa.

"Quat," the Egyptian doctor said to me. He had an air of resignation.

He added,

"Like many others, the boy may have a relapse. Quat is stronger than anything. Stronger than us doctors. There should be preventative education in schools, community centers, clinics . . ."

Quat isn't only Satan at your mouth, but it's also the devil at your wallet. A Yemenite spends one third of his income on his drug

Chewing quat balls make a balloon grow in your cheek and your eyes pop out.

habit. Next to the price of quat our bottle of red costs nothing. Quat is the gold standard of Yemen. The ups and downs of the quat's Dow Jones decide the family budget and ultimately determine its well-being.

The Sanaa newspaper *Al Thawra (The Revolution)* did its own survey. "Every quat addict squanders an average of 100 rials a day. This doesn't include the quat he gives to his friends . . ." The writer asks his readers to give the subject some serious thought, "If you saved these 100 rials a day, in one year you could buy a plot of land, add two rooms to your house, buy a car or take a luxury vacation abroad."

Quat is a hard nugget for the Yemenite government to chew. Those who try to throw a wrench into this formidable industry, fail. Entire tribes, big land-owners, common peasants, transporters, sellers and middlemen live off the quat crop. The smallest quat dealer doesn't earn more than 50 rials a day. Yet by inflating his cheek every afternoon, he slowly deflates his stomach. And once his stomach is contracted, so is hunger and the need for food money.

Quat isn't a drug sold "under the table." It's sold on the ground at streetcorners or literally on the table of tiny shops in the "quat district." Sometimes these shops consist of nothing more than a big wooden box placed into a hole in the wall for the seller to sit on. In front of him is a high table on stilts extending the box's surface into the alley. It's the counter. Quat, the green dream-weaver, is heaped everywhere in bundles and piles, overflowing the table tops. These shops are in long rows, like rabbit cages where man replaces rabbit and quat replaces clover. The bargaining is heated. The quat addict is a connoisseur. He knows every subtle detail to determine the quality and price of his beloved plant.

The Press Goes to War

The increase of quat is linked to emigration. In 1970 Yemen finally opened up to the world. Since then emigration has increased continuously, bringing an influx of cash and the expanding quat crops. The emigrant who returns with his pockets full of money doesn't want to wear himself out anymore working the fields. He hires a field hand, stoned on quat, who demands an exorbitant salary for a very short day.

The villages are emptied of their men, the fields of their tillers. Quat grows wild year round. A lucrative harvest. With one shrub of quat you earn twenty times more than you would from a coffee

tree. The average revenue of 2½ acres of quat went from 7,000 to

10,000 rials between 1960 and 1970. In 1981 in the Hajja region, it allegedly reached 134,000 rials.

Little by little the drug encroaches on arable land, stealing valuable space in this favorable climate where so many other crops could grow and flourish. Coffee has for centuries been the trademark of Yemen and its main resource. Today its aroma is vanishing. So is the infamous grape celebrated by so many poets. Fruits and vegetables are imported now from Egypt and Lebanon. Today it's easier to find a lemon at the North Pole than in Yemen. Unregulated prices climb to absurd heights.

To ease their conscience about quat, some Yemenites argue:

"Quat isn't so bad for the nation. The emigrants' money is used for buying quat, so it stays in the country and supplies the banks. Not only that, the money gets channeled from the cities into the rural areas, so the peasants don't leave their villages looking for work."

To raise Yemenites' consciousness, *Al Thawra* writes,

"Quat is our social disease, but making it illegal will not heal us. We have to replace it with other entertainment: books, theatre or sports. We have to develop our agricultural cooperatives and create industries. We no longer produce, all we do is consume, tastelessly, greedily, never thinking further than the next day." The article continues, "The Chinese have found the formula to wake up the people and rid themselves of opium. Why can't we get rid of quat?"

In 1976, the former People's Republic of South Yemen took measures making the consumption of the drug illegal except on weekends. When this law was, alas, repealed some twelve or thirteen years later, there were heated protests to this change among the South Yemenites who believed the proscription of the drug had been a good idea.

At the Caravanserai, the Traditional Inn

It's evening in Sanaa at the Bab-el-Yemen market, not far from the quat souk. I stumble, there's a loud clattering noise. As the road to hell is paved with good intentions so the streets of Yemen are paved with imported cans.

Hundreds of cats with golden eyes follow me everywhere, staring at me from the market walls. Is this an ad campaign meant for the owners of the undernourished felines lurking in the darkness *109* of streets and alleys? Is it touting a can of Pretty Whiskers, Purr or Meow? No. The golden-eyes extol the virtues of a battery. Black-outs are common here, some streets still have no streetlights; flashlights are essential.

Other eyes glimmer above the narrow streets submerged in darkness; these stained-glass windows of all colors glint from the facades of high houses that touch shoulder to shoulder. Walking at night in Bab-el-Yemen is like being an ant wandering inside Aladdin's magic lamp. I go through the spice-market; scents filter through closed wooden shutters. I feel a flutter of wings brush against me; the veil of a woman hurrying home after the last load of water for the day.

A wall suddenly lights up—a door is opened wide onto the alley. It's a hotel, a caravanserai where pilgrims stop on their way to Mecca. They no longer travel with the caravans and camels of the

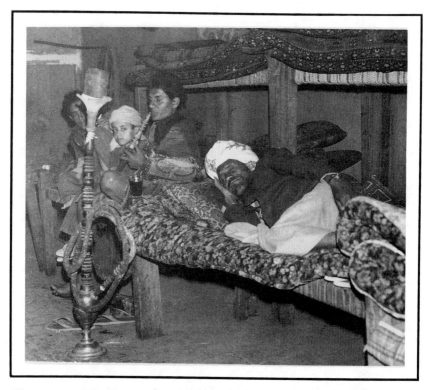

The ancient caravanserais* are very cheap but you have to sleep all together on bunk beds in a large common room. (See glossary)

old days but by bus and plane. They're from Yemen's provinces. Here, forty or fifty men spend the night in a large common room under a high deep, sea-blue ceiling. They lie on hard iron beds or the woven rope of wooden bunks. Wide aisles separate the scaffolding of the bunk beds piled on top of one another all the way up to the ceiling. The sleepers' heads laid out on shelves, framed by the wooden structures and rounded out by their turbans, resemble apples laid out on trays, waiting to ripen. But their aroma is different.

I look all around the room.

"No women! Where do the women sleep? Don't they also make the pilgrimage?"

A man points his finger to the ceiling.

"Up there on the second floor."

Just next door at the corner cafe are the pilgrims who haven't gone to sleep yet. The cafe is splashed with color, so different from the gloom of our Western bus and train stations. As you enter, you see a huge stone that dominates the room. This naturally rounded out wavy form, painted gentian-blue against an apple-green wall, is a giant furnace. Its belly a hollowed out deep, glowing, red cavity; the hearth is fed with dry branches and roots.

Three men are lying on top of this primitive stove. Intertwined with the tubes of water pipes, they lean on their elbows. The ceiling just above their heads is the only thing that keeps them from flying off in a cloud of smoke. "Stored" quat deforms their cheeks. The chewers are obviously so far from the floor and down-to-earth matters that I, the journalist, will have to look elsewhere for interviews.

I sit at a rickety iron table and order the traditional tea served in little glasses. It's very strong and sweet and burns your tongue and fingers. A man approaches, examining me. He looks fragile. His temple is covered with a white bandage. He's cut off the sleeves of a tweed jacket to make a vest.

"Where're you from?" he asks.

"From Switzerland. What about you?"

"My name is Mohammed Nasser. I've come from Djebel Yazid near Amran to get treated at the military hospital here in Sanaa. But the other customers here are all pilgrims; their next stop is the airport. I'm sleeping at the inn next door. One night costs 10 rials, but if you're only staying for a little nap, a waterpipe smoke or a quat party, it's 5 rials."

The purveyors of quat come around mid-day to deliver it on the market place. The leaves have been cut at dawn and must be chewed without delay.

Women selling bread. The traditional Yemenite bread is thin, round and delicious. Women bake it at home. Then, piled up on a round shaped tray which they carry on their heads, they sell it on the streets.

Foreign Luxuries

Ten rials a night! I spend thirty times that much for a hotel on the main street—it's modern but still decorated Yemenite style with mosaic and stucco lace. Yemenite customers have to leave their "jambia" at the front desk, yet they can keep the dagger sheath on their belt.

Between the cheap but clean caravanserais and the luxury hotels, there are, alas, allegedly modern establishments with stained wall to wall carpets and pipes duly plugged up. But for the chicest of chic you go to the top-rated American hotels. Imported from top to bottom, financed by oil barons of the Arabian gulf, managed by foreigners, decorated with fake Van Goghs, fed with frozen chicken, sprinkled with alcohol, equipped with swimming pools, conference rooms, melodious elevators, throbbing stereos, psyche-delic dance floors whirling with pink and blue lights.

These massive foreign growths sprout up with their heads in the clouds and feet in the dust. If you want to be understood there you had better speak English. The State is poor but money is everywhere. A square foot of land in the center of Sanaa is worth the same as in Paris or New York. Sanaa also has its builders and speculators.

Yet production is low. Yemen imports almost everything. In-dustry is somnolent. For years there were only a few factories, namely two textile companies established by the Chinese near Sanaa and a few small sites near Taiz, producing candy, furniture, foam rubber and plastics. Plans were made for an aluminum factory, "the biggest in the Arab world." For the time being the people just joke: "Yemen is the poorest richest and most expensive country!"

Two Egyptians, dressed in their traditional robes, with rustic faces, said to me in the plane which took me from Cairo to Sanaa,

"We're masons. We'll earn ten times more working in Yemen than a bureaucrat does in Egypt."

Zaidites and Shaffeites

At the Sheraton the telephone switchboard buzzes. But for the guests of the Bab-el-Yemen caravanserai the Arab word-of-mouth telephone suffices. News and information come, go, wander by foot, bus, truck, or shared taxi among poultry and guns. They guide the pilgrims along the path which crosses the Yemenite border until the pilgrims finally reach the Sacred Black Stone, the Kaaba in

Mecca. The Yemenite government only allows a single pass for Mecca. With a real passport pilgrims might want to stay there. Under the guise of faith, Yemenites search for work in Saudi Arabia, the land of black gold.

In the green and blue cafe, next to the ten-rial-a-night hotel, a group of pilgrims are having a huddle. The unrelenting female interrogator doesn't hesitate to enter the cluster of turbans.

"Where're you from?" I ask.

"From Dhamar between Taiz and Sanaa."

"Are you Zaidite or Shaffeite?"

The difference between a Zaidite and Shaffeite isn't any more apparent here than is the difference between a Protestant or Catholic in the West. They look the same except for small details on their turbans or slight differences in accents. The Zaidites, a Shiite sect founded in the ninth century, live on the high plateaus of Yemen's mountains. The Shaffeites, a sect also founded in the ninth century, practice a religion which is very close to Sunnite. Yemen also is host to some Ismaelians whose leader is Aga Khan.

In the cafe one of my interrogated pilgrim-quat addicts spits green and replies,

"Zaidite or Shaffeite, what difference does it make! We pray in the same mosques!"

Nonetheless, someone feels the need to add,

"Our group is Zaidite!"

Warriors and Businessmen

The journalist and her victims are sitting on low, folding, metal chairs, once painted but now rusted.

The curious cluster around us. At eye-level I see short skirts forming a wall of twiggy legs whose knee-high socks keep sliding down. A man suddenly steps back, stands up straight, and turns toward me.

"Look!"

To show me he lets his arms hang down, hands pressed against his thighs:

"We Zaidites pray like this!"

"And the Shaffeites?"

A skinny little man steps forward and sets his hands one on top of the other at the front of his large belt.

114   "We pray like this!"

Anxious to talk, the man next to him impatiently elbows his way forward.

"No Shaffeite has ever been King of Yemen. All Imams were Zaidite, all were descendants of the great Ali."

"That's true," admits the skinny one. "Being close to Sunnites, we Shaffeites never considered the Iman more than the ruler of Yemen. But for Zaidites, the King was vested with God's will. To go against the King was to go against religion, and going against religion is a serious offense."

He chuckles.

"Yes, the Zaidites are warriors but we Shaffeites are good businessmen. There're fewer Shaffeites, but like the sea we live next to, we have wide open minds. Shaffeites' minds aren't closed in by the mountains or dusted with the sand."

"Where do Shaffeites live?"

"Along the Red Sea, in the Tihama plain, in Hodeyda, Taiz and Aden. I myself come from Aden. When the English were there education was more advanced than in the North in the Imam's kingdom. The Zaidite kingdom only had a few schools which always had the same teachings from the Koran."

Shaffeites, because of the relative liberalism of their religion, their openness and their education, are not only businessmen, but often executives in government and military administration. There are also many diplomats among them.

After having praised the qualities of his people, my skinny Shaffeite diplomatically declares,

"Shaffeites and Zaidites are brothers. There's only one God."

The Price of the Holy Voyage

There is only one God, but there are innumerable agents who promise pilgrims to bring them to Him. Many are crooks. Business is good in the business of faith. Too good, declare the Sanaa newspapers.

During the frantic month of pilgrimage to Mecca, Yemenite and Saudi airlines have six or seven flights a day, sometimes more. Even though the pilgrims are packed in, there are always more left in the waiting rooms. More tickets are sold than there are seats.

The Sanaa airport, ten miles from the city, was designed by West German architects and engineers, a rare example of traditional architecture gracefully adapted to needs of the modern world. Stained glass windows decorate the main lobby. Sanaa's control tower looks like a minaret. Why not a gothic bell tower for Parisian airports?

The airport grows and continues to spread in a wild landscape scattered with black volcanic rocks. It's November. Dawn awakens. The light takes on an intangible purple. From far-away mosques, muezzins' chants are carried on gusts of wind. I shiver. Intonations of the human voice calling for prayer in Islam touch me far more than the tolling bronze bells of Christianity.

In certain Yemenite mosques, the muezzin's daily recitations are taped and automatically played five times a day at prayer. In others, the muezzin still chants himself, but his heart and legs can rest thanks to modern technology; he broadcasts from downstairs through a microphone, delivering his divine message without having to climb the steep minaret stairs all the way to the top.

In the airport lobby, pilgrims are everywhere, lying on small rugs with heads resting on a bundle, or curled up on a seat. There are thousands of them sleeping wrapped in their pieces of cloth and rolled up in blankets. Once they're awake, like a flock of white lambs getting up, you see white veils emerge, and slowly everything turns to whiteness. White is the color of pilgrimage. You go to Mecca dressed in a single immaculate cloth, symbolizing humility and the equality of all men before God. Outside the airport lobby, just before sunrise I see men lining themselves up. Torsos naked in the brisk air, they pray facing Mecca.

Women pilgrims cover their faces out of custom, but sometimes it serves certain purposes. At age fifty, a woman can hide behind her veil to take advantage of the special airfares reserved for groups under age twenty-five.

With the Spirit of God

The pilgrims are happy no matter what happens to them on earth: the snacks costing ten times the normal price, the planes leaving without them, all the thievery of vultures who make a kingdom of profit out of the Prophet's country! Yet the pilgrims are at peace, the Spirit is with them.

An elder travels with his little tin kettle, painted blue. He's been waiting for a week.

"But I'll be leaving with God's help!"

A woman travels with tuberculosis, one of the plagues of Yemen.

"I live in the cool shade of happiness, Allah will heal me."

Zaidites and Shaffeites share their influence on Yemen and pray in the same mosques.

Sanaa airport is flooded with pilgrims at the time of the hadj*, the month of pilgrimage to Mecca. (See glossary)

The hours slide over the patient crowd. Suddenly a wave ripples through them; the loudspeaker has announced a departure for Djeddah, the next step on the hazardous road to God. They hastily gather their belongings and feverishly wave their documents. They hurry, they worry: "Is it finally my turn?" For those who've never left their village the pilgrimage is an adventure. Rial after rial has been patiently saved for the Holy Voyage.

Having passed the passport and ticket checkpoints I resort to my fins to go upstream like a salmon. The human wave crushes me, lifting me to the wrong gate. I don't have a rendezvous north with Allah in Saudi Arabia, I have one south in the Yemenite Republic's fine city of Taiz! Praise be to God and bless the Heavens, I finally make my way through the obstacle course and find the right gate, the right plane and the right seat. The plane is almost empty. Tonight on its return flight, it'll be full of southern pilgrims, like a souk market before Friday.

God is with the pilgrims, but today the gods are with me. Yemen Airways leaves right on time! Morning light suddenly is upon us. The airport, the sky, the earth and mountains are crystal clear as if the night had polished the whole landscape.

My plane lifts off. Through a porthole I see the moving white mass of pilgrims on the runway as the first batch rushes into the belly of the big bird. From up in the sky Yemenite soldiers, already so small, become even smaller. I once mistook these airport guards for armed children.

The Intellectuals

While adults are flying away on Boeings, the children of Sanaa go round and round on a carousel plane painted with daisies, squeeking and wobbling under a rusted roof. Luna Park is the newest thrill for little kids. But older children prefer the immemorial Yemenite game: shooting. Crouched on the sidewalks downtown, they use old rifles to shoot at cigarettes or rotten eggs precariously set on shaky cardboard boxes.

The children of Sanaa also have their "intellectuals." One can see them sitting on sidewalks, their noses buried in books brushing against the skirts of passersby. I remember a completely absorbed trio squeezed together against a wall, oblivious to the world around them. The first one was droning out the Holy Koran, the other two were immersed in comics translated into Arabic—Tarzan and Barbarella.

In front of the mosque in Liberation Square, public scribes, parked under umbrellas, await their clientele. The legs of their iron tables are planted in the dusty, beaten earth. There are usually two or three of them, sometimes more. The best one has earned his reputation from his fine calligraphy and his art of beautiful prose. He also knows Islamic law and is somewhat of a lawyer. No one can compose a visa or administrative request better than he. No one can make an appeal to a ministry's decision or plead for a certificate of good character with his finesse.

Sheltered by the huge lampshade of his umbrella, fringes casting a purple shadow on his papers, the public scribe eloquently elaborates upon the thoughts and wishes of those who come to him. While he writes he recites aloud what has been said to him by his client, adding his own lyricism. Sometimes the knight of the plume freezes his pen in mid-air, lowers his glasses to the tip of his nose, peering over them to gauge his client:

"You're forty aren't you?"

Sometimes the man will correct the scribe; often, though, he keeps quiet because he doesn't really know how old he is. From now on the scribe's estimate will be considered his official age.

The traditional public scribe, a literate and a lively storyteller, is also modern. On his iron table he carefully lines up the luxurious accessories indispensable for the perfect correspondent: a stapler, a hole puncher and a Parker pen. Next to this equipment a little glass of steaming hot tea is regularly emptied and then refilled.

It's been some time since everyone's man of letters has used carbon copies. Now if his client wants a document copied, the scribe sends him to a nearby shop. A shop which looks like all of the other traditional shops except that it proudly displays the latest in xeroxing, enlarging, and reducing technology.

The distinguished public writers, inheriting of a long tradition, now have their competitors: amateurs and students seated in the unshaded dust in front of the post office, on the lookout for potential customers and a few rials.

Buying and Selling

Further down the street, stores display everything and anything from everywhere. From the best buy to the most over-priced, from the most practical to the flashiest and most useless junk. You can

Abashed and deafened by the racket of engines, the peasant lost his way: things are moving too fast in Sanaa!

get highly supportive brassieres or high-fidelity stereos, you can get powder to powder your nose or powder to do your laundry, you can get plain wall paint for your house or sophisticated face paints from New York and Paris.

In front of these tempting shop windows, people push past street vendors who once sold water and peanuts, but now sell Coca Cola and chewing gum. Some of them sell the popular modern magic lantern, a slide viewer where you slip in a little round cardboard wheel with a dozen tourist cliches on it. You can travel through pictures far beyond Yemen's Red Sea by simply turning the wheel.

Sanaa's tree vendors sit on the pavement of traffic islands. They stoically swallow the dust and attempt to sell long flexible sticks which they claim will someday grow leaves.

The streets of Sanaa are full of turbans and veils, but you can also come across the three-piece suit of Yemenite Yuppies. In their haste, will they know how to build Yemen without destroying it? They rush through the city gripping attache cases, dressed in businessmen's costumes from which protrude their rounded bellies. Their short stature is often boosted by Italian platform shoes.

For some the shoe means progress . . . and moving up. Shoes sell well in Yemen. Once, in the Imam's country, most Yemenites went barefoot.

One day on my way to the town of Ibb, I noticed what at first glance looked to be a former market, plopped along the side of the road. Consisting of a few clay-mound shops built between two villages, there was not even a stray cat wandering about. Walking through "the market," I suddenly came upon hundreds of shoes, piled up five feet high in the sand at the end of the path. Full of holes, and deformed from being worn too big on feet too small, they gave off a strong smell of burnt leather. The sight awakened my European guilt complex, for in my mind's eye I again saw those horrifying images: the mountains of clothes, shoes, crutches, artificial limbs and glasses which had belonged to the Nazis' last victims in the concentration camps, grim evidence filmed by the liberators before the Nazis had had time to burn it in their ovens.

Fashion Labels from the West

But, here in Yemen, there are no horrors, no genocide. Only shoes are liquidated—not people. Why bother repairing the old stuff when the new is so appealing? And in this country, "the poorest, richest and most expensive," the new is lavishly displayed in the shop windows of big cities: Italian shirts Via Veneto style with assorted cufflinks, pure silk French shirts, ties and bow ties, cashmere sweaters from Scotland, fine suits from Milano or Turin and accessories for tennis snobs who never play tennis and yachtsmen who never navigate the seas.

The merchandise of luxury boutiques, often brought through Saudi Arabia, carry genuine designer labels. In the souks, however, imitations sell—and sell well. Christian Dior made in Taiwan becomes Christian Dior*e*. Fashionable Yemenites aren't only partial to clothes, they also love cologne. The best of Dior, Lanvin, Saint-Laurent and Guy Laroche is imported to Yemen.

Japan Makes Its Way onto the Streets

The outdoor barber in Liberation Square doesn't bother with foreign fragrances. A cheap musk suffices as the finishing touch to his shaves. He sets up shop on a single chair which leans against the wall of the mosque. His tools are either on the ground or in his pockets: a tin bowl, a bar of soap, a big shaving brush, a genuine old-fashioned shaving blade, a leather knife-sharpener, some dusty towels, an old tin pitcher and his bottle of poor-man's perfume.

Facing the mosque, a troupe of auto-taxis lines up, while a battalion of moto-taxis revs its engines. A moto-taxi doesn't cost much and can wind its way through the narrowest of back alleys, but if you decide to ride one you will have a blue behind and be drowned in dust.

Suzuki, Kawasaki, Honda, Toyota, Mazda. Japan has conquered ancient Yemen, which, only yesterday, still had to settle for horse shoes. West Germany, the U.S. and France are coasting far behind. On the city streets, torn up though they had just been paved, you hear the constant racket of honking, rumbling and backfiring.

The Yemenite loves to dote over his motorcycle. Garlands, pompoms, ribbons, feathers, plastic fruits and flowers, decals of black panthers, tropical birds and arctic bears, all decorate the anatomy of his beloved. Blond Nestle's babies and movie stars smile from the fenders.

Heavy trucks coming from Saudi Arabia are also brightened up with colorful motifs. The kitsch white-sails-floating-on-a-nordic-lake pictures painted on their sides are common, cooling the scorching metal of these modern camels. Some proudly display the saber of the Saudi Arabian kingdom's coat of arms.

Roll 'Em

In the center of the square are all manner and form of public transportation. Not only moto-taxis and auto-taxis, but shared taxis, local minibuses and buses meant to cross thousands of miles of desert. Next to all this the photo peddler parks his decor set up on a bicycle, operating in the heat and dust. This unique photographer has created a portable full-size photo studio. His clients are travelers, emigration applicants or returned emigrants applying for marriage, and families—minus women of course. They all pose for him in front of the photo studio curtain above which he's suspended a Garden of Eden, a crescent shaped paradise in plastic with an abundance of leaves tacked with lemons, oranges and naturally, the fatal apple. Set on top of the entire fandango is a red rubber fish swimming at the tip of the highest leaf. This paradise on bicycle arrives every morning, never leaving until sundown.

The waiting period for pictures is short since the artist uses a Polaroid (in color). While husbands, boys and little girls stand in front of the camera and the curtain, women and adolescent girls watch the scene from behind their curtain of veils.

Like their peers in Washington and Paris, the Chiefs of the Yemenite State have their portraits taken too, but in private, of course. And the kids of Sanaa snatch up a few rials selling the pictures in Liberation Square, in the souk or on the street—even when the original is no longer on the political scene.

Not far from the photo peddler, a more ambitious, better equipped photographer has set up shop. He shoots his customers against a painted canvas background with greek columns, a blue sky and an even bluer sea; you would think you were in a turn of the century studio. But a little farther down on the main street you return to the space age, finding shop windows full of the most sophisticated photo equipment. Yet, few know how to focus the complex lenses and even fewer shops can properly develop film or fix a camera.

Coins and "Foutas"

To acquire these wonders you have to have money . . . which isn't lacking in Yemen. You feel it everywhere. It stuffs Yemenite pockets front and back, inflating their shabby jackets. For many Yemenites looking poor is just an appearance—except of course for those who are truly destitute, beggars and the physically or mentally handicapped.

Money is piled up on shop counters right in the middle of the street, they pass it from hand to hand, right in the middle of a crowd. In the bank I came across an old man. He laughed, seeing my surprise before the tower of bills placed on the counter within everyone's reach. With his finger pointed at the wads of money piled up brick by brick, like a typical Yemenite minaret, he said.

"Yes, we're trustworthy, but for how long, unh?"

After collecting all the bills into his skirt, like a farm woman gathering eggs into her apron, the elder left with a quick, light step.

The Main Street money changer is proud of his machine. The machine frees his hands, tired of so many business and monetary transactions. It counts the bills as fast as the wind sweeps the desert. The man is practical and only accepts the universal American dollar. He also has a sense of humor:

"I can trust my machine. She never makes a mistake and isn't susceptible to temptations . . . I don't have to keep an eye on her."

The loyal machine cost 12,000 rials—peanuts for a money changer who's shrewd and Yemenite.

Another machine purrs two shops away at the laundromat. Its enormous stomach gobbles up all kinds of men's jackets: new or old, baggy or fitted, plaid or checkered, wool or cotton, tweed or velvet, drab or colorful, pink or aqua green. Or . . . the electric blue of the jacket which a migrant brought back from the U.S. He proudly wears the magnificent blue turban he made to match it.

Pants are few among these jackets. The majority of Yemenites still wear a skirt, hand washed at home. These "foutas" are mid-length wrap-around skirts, imported or made domestically. The color white predominates in the north of Yemen. The closer you get to the center of the country especially towards the south, the livelier the colors get. Fabrics from Asia imitate Scottish plaids, but with full rich colors: turquoise blue, jade green, shocking pink or marigold. Some with more tender skin, seeking plush elegance, wrap themselves in a brightly colored bath towel, holding it up with a leather belt. In the north most men wear the long Arab robe.

Among the customers packed into the drycleaner's, a man is waiting for his jacket to be pressed. He's made himself comfortable, taking off his belt and dagger. Set on the ground, they don't leave his sight. A full-blooded Yemenite treasures his "jambia" more than anything. The oldest and most beautiful ones have a handle made 125

Thousands of trucks shuttle between Yemen and the Near-East. Many are decorated with pictures of Mecca. And sometimes with dreamlike landscapes; white sailing boats and blue lakes bring an illusion of coolness to the scorching metal.

Money changers in Saada, the city in the far north of Yemen. Displayed on a piece of cloth are not only bills, but also cartridges, daggers, silver coins and jewelry.

Two accountants at work in one of the branches of the Indochina and Suez Bank. Hold-ups haven't yet been imported to Yemen.

Yemen has printed bills only since 1964. The Development and Reconstruction Bank of Yemen was built on Liberation Square next to one of the King's ancient palaces—now transformed into a museum. The bank's design fits harmoniously with the palace's traditional architecture.

of either giraffe or rhinoceros horn—rhino horn allegedly enhances sexual powers hence the demand that is decimating the African rhino population.

These handles made of horn are considered even more precious than the beautiful inlaid or filigreed Yemenite silver sheaths. In high-ranking families, the "jambia" is passed down from generation to generation—a priceless heirloom. I know of a jambia which was valued at $200,000.

Getting to Matters of the Palate

At the corner cafe I again run into the money changer. We share a bottle of Coca-Cola and our views on Yemenite cuisine. The day before I relished the finest Yemenite dishes in the elegant restaurant of Bab-el-Gaa Square.

But typical Yemenite restaurants are much less elaborate: a few folding chairs and some tables, often set on a beaten earth floor. The menu is simple. Chicken is prepared the modern way, browned and rotated on an electric roaster. But beans are cooked the old-fashioned way, simmering all day in a giant, sooty black cauldron set over a wood-burning fire. The cook's face is red over the heat, the flames reflecting on his wet skin. With a long stick he stirs the thick mass which looks like a witch's brew but is actually delicious, especially when seasoned with tomatoes, onions and peppers.

In some cities a few restaurants add Near East dishes to their menu: meatballs, rice, ratatouille, lentil soup, and the typical Egyptian "molokheya" which is a kind of spinach, prepared as a stew with pieces of lamb or chicken. To top off a spicy meal, sweet puddings made with milk or cream of wheat and blended with raisins are served for dessert.

Some places provide forks with the usual spoon but generally you eat with your fingers, sliding the food into little round, flat pita pouches. Alas, these delicious little wheels are becoming scarce with the importation of mass produced white bread sliced into loaves. This standard bread is tasteless, but easy to preserve. Genuine traditional Yemenite bread is twice as expensive. It's a large, round, thin pancake which dries out fast. There are no bakeries in Yemen; women knead and bake the bread at home, then sell it on the streets.

The local coffee shops have become home for plastic and tin: thermoses, water pitchers, cups, plates and trays all made in Hong Kong. Here and there one can still find some beautiful antique

In Sanaa's modern hotels, the traveler enjoys all modern conveniences plus some avant-garde gadgets. They are very expensive.

samovars; with wooden grips or handles, they are tall, round, silver-colored kettles where tea ripples all day long. Alas, the aroma of traditional finely ground tea leaves, served in little glasses, doesn't waft through public places like it used to. Today, you have to settle for teabags steeped in plastic cups.

Nevertheless these places are inviting. Coming in from the hot dusty street, you see walls painted aqua green and sea blue, making you feel like you're plunging into the coolness of an underwater cave. On these walls, between Seven-Up posters and verses of the Koran, "Made in China" cuckoo clocks which haven't had a single cuckoo pop out in years, keep time.

The Yemenite chef doesn't bother wearing the chef's uniform of a white apron and pyramid chef's hat. He covers himself with a plastic Donald Duck apron to match his synthetic equipment. Yet his embroidered skullcap and the old thick walls of his cafe remind you of times of yore. This place is the meeting of modern and ancient; it's always full.

A Variety of Cuisine

The Kentucky Fried Chicken restaurant is almost empty. The true Yemenite would gladly eat out of a plastic plate, but seemingly will not eat plastic on his plate! He disdains frozen chicken, rubbery sandwiches, mushy french fries with ketchup. You won't see many turbans beneath the trademark portrait of the founder of this famous chain: a grandaddy image with rosy cheeks, a goatee, a mustache and a bolo tie. As for the ice cream and popcorn vendor, he does good business with ice cream but not with the inflated grain of corn. Alas, someday business may improve since Yemen's new generation likes this americana too much.

Not long ago Yemenites had a limited selection of food, if any. Today you can find Chateaubriand steaks "à la française," Vietnamese chicken, Cantonese rice and more. As the city of Sanaa continues to expand, so does the variety of cuisine.

Chinese Lamb

Sitting on a rock overlooking the capital is . . . a red Chinese-laquered pagoda! Built years ago as a memorial to the Chinese doctors, engineers and workers who died in Yemen, today the pagoda shades Yemenite dreamers, poets and picnickers.

But the Chinese in Yemen don't only minister to people's health, build homes, or pave roads; they've opened up a restaurant. Just as Mississippi lags behind New York by a few seasons, so the Great Chinese Restaurant of Sanaa lags many moons behind Beijing. The management isn't up with the times. Here history is at a standstill; the U.S. still hasn't entered the gates of the Great Wall of China to undermine Maoist austerity. The atmosphere is gloomy, in spite of the red scarlet columns, the pom-pommed red and black lamps, and the pink and blue plastic hummingbirds buzzing around fake flowers.

The comrade waiters and waitresses drag around in their worn uniforms among dirty tables. They take your order in spite of themselves, indifferently give it to the cook and obliviously toss it at you. Chinese food, elsewhere known for its subtle qualities, is bland here—as bland as the impersonal eyes of the personnel, as bland as the gaze of the comrade-cashier sitting stiffly behind his table with his cup of green tea decorated with a blue fish.

And yet the Chinese of Sanaa haven't hesitated to use capitalist, televised advertising to laud the Great Restaurant's service and delicacies. Some Yemenites have let themselves be taken in. One of them sitting at the table to my left, lifts his eyes from his plate, looks at me and makes a face, obviously disgusted with the food. My newly found gourmet friend contemptuously pushes his plate away, leaving it half full, then says:

"Nope, this Chinese lamb is just not as good as our Yemenite lamb!"

I burst out laughing.

"They won't take you in again, huh? Real Yemenites aren't sheep!"

My play on words quickly makes the rounds of the room.

The man sitting to my right is old and blind in one eye, but with his good eye he laughs for two. A few minutes later he introduces himself:

"My name is Saleh Al-Ouswali. I'm mayor of Haraf Soufyan at the north of Yemen. This young man next to me is the director of our local development center."

Water and Woman

The two men let themselves be taken in by the televised aroma of Chinese food—though they've obviously come to the capital, first and foremost, on business. They're having problems:

131

"For us water is life. Our peasants dug a well and poured the cement, but now it's up to the State to lay the pipes to the village. We've come to Sanaa to meet one of the directors of the Ministry of Public Works. We're going to ask him to move up the date for the work, which isn't supposed to begin for another six months. For the time being, water is being brought to the school and medical center by truck. Transporting the water is expensive, it costs almost a rial a gallon."

The mayor calls on my sense of female solidarity.

"Our women go back and forth from house to well, from well to house, all day long. It's exhausting. Being a woman, you should sympathize."

I opt for a teasing feminism.

"I sympathize, I sympathize, but I've got a better solution. Send the men for water!"

The mayor travels the middle road, he's a pacifist.

"That's a good idea. But by the time I'll have convinced the men to do the women's work, the State will have already laid the pipes!"

Even though he's of the younger generation, the director of the development center is aghast at my sexist suggestion. He tries to set things straight.

"To tell you the truth, it isn't the State who's behind schedule, we're the ones ahead of schedule. We were so impatient to have water that we worked faster than usual."

Since 1975 hundreds of cooperatives and development centers have been established in North Yemen. These collective organizations also act as communication links; their representatives are Sanaa's best "ambassadors" to the rural areas.

At the beginning, touchy tribal chiefs, thinking that their power was threatened, pulled out their guns. But today, drawn by the honey of progress, many among them support the State development program. Only some Sheikhs of the "great fierce north" still refuse to collaborate ... all the while complaining of a lack of roads, water and electricity.

The Development Centers

These development centers were not established as Western-style cooperatives or Soviet-style communes. Their role was to inform and guide the peasants, propose programs and provide the means
132 to fulfill them with selected seed, tractors and modern equipment.

Modern equipment is now replacing the mule, horse or camel, but you still come across caravans carrying wood on camel back. Wood was as rare as water in Yemen, hence endless fights among the tribes.

Until they came, the Yemenite peasant knew only of the mule, horse and camel. Patiently, he climbed clinging to the slopes of his terraced crops in the mountain coolness. Stoically, he bent over against the winds of the plains in the lowlands' sweltering heat. He knew nothing of the tractor or the harvester-thresher.

Financing for the development centers is partially assured by the religious tax, "the zaakat." Sanaa uses 75% of this tax for development. The cooperatives also receive foreign grants, technical assistance from more developed countries, and some practical and financial support from the peasants themselves.

The Weight of Feudalism

In one village, the director of the development center told me that the locals paid for half the cost of treating and pumping water.

"When people pay for it out of their own pockets they're much more willing to cooperate. They take better care of the equipment and work harder."

All these new projects look good on paper and they work in certain regions and certain situations. But the archaic land tenure system in northern Yemen has slowed down the progress many Yemenites had been hoping for. Here, as in Europe not so long ago, the poor provide the labour and the rich provide the land and water. The peasant owes a third of his harvest, sometimes more, to his landowner. His budget is strained by yet another tax—the "tenth of a quarter" of his harvest as is stated in the Koran, which he gives as he can in like or kind. He also has to pay for seed to plant his crops.

These are among the reasons for the continuous emigration, the enrollment of twelve year old boys in the Army and the abandonment of fields, left to be worked in by women, children and by old men.

Near Taiz, a mile from the main road, Al-Gond is slowly falling into ruin. The village lies still, suffocated by the sun. The round curves of a mosque's domes built in the time of the Prophet, are among its only remains. Next to these remains I met a potter who worked as his ancestors must have done thousands of years ago; he knew nothing of the potter's wheel and exhausted himself turning round and round his clay pot. Yet Al Gond is the silent, timeless place which has allegedly been set aside for the raising of genuine Yemenite chickens, Yemen's loudest industry.

Not far from Al Gond, I stopped to visit Ti Sofal, a region where they grow mainly the "dora" crop—a kind of corn Yemenites use for bread flour. In the distance a ploughman worked his field, his camel pulling the hoe. In Ti-Sofal the air was soft and the shade cool under thin small trees, their silver leaves trembling in the wind. The director of the development center bragged,

"See these trees, I just planted them! I'm going to make a public garden out of this place. Before it was a graveyard. See over there! We're going to have a soccer field and sports facilities."

Encounters with Development

The FAO (the United Nations' Food and Agriculture Organization) launched the enormous undertaking of irrigation and development. They drew up plans for the construction of several dams throughout the scorching Tihama plains, in the region near the ancient city of Zebid. Their hope was to root the peasants to the land and prevent the exodus from continuing. It wasn't easy! According to sacro-sanct United Nations principles, not a single project can be initiated without the approval of local authorities. And here the authorities, the big landowners, weren't enthusiastic about relinquishing the water distribution rights they had always controlled.

At first the peasants around Zebid in "capitalist" North Yemen were afraid of their land being seized and collectivized, as in the neighboring People's Democratic Republic of Yemen. These Zebid peasants took to their arms to prevent the workers from entering one of the dam construction sites; they finally put down their guns with the help of a few rials. Once the work finally did begin there were other problems. One peasant had an unpleasant encounter with insecticides. When an FAO representative strapped a large insecticide spray canister to his back, the poor man fled in full gear, terrified of the machine vibrating his body. Another peasant refused to kill the ravaging insects because they were "creatures of God." From their mosques, the religious leaders cried: "Communism!". For them, the FAO project was the work of the devil.

But time has passed. Much water has run through the dams spread out like a string of prayer beads along the Tihama plains. The most adamant farmer no longer hesitates to use the spray-murder machine. He rents it and when he can, he buys it. The plants flourish after the treatment. The peasants are delighted.

CHAPTER FIVE

A Dozen Women in a Taxi Aren't Worth One Man

Beneath the skies of China, Mao Tse-tung once said: "Women are half the sky."

In most of Yemen, this "half the sky" is hidden behind a cloud. Thick or transparent, black or in color, this cloud is the veil. But times are slowly changing. To veil or not to veil, that is the question. Some women, though very few, have answered by changing their veil into scarves. They still cover their heads and hide their hair, but the cloud over their faces is gone. Finally, their eyes are alive. It is said that eyes are the mirror of the soul. But for me, eyes peering out from between two pieces of cloth reflect nothing without the expression of eyebrows, a mouth, a pout or a smile. They are only eyes.

Male students were among those who initiated change. They were no longer afraid of being harassed by people who felt the need to split hairs by attacking the "long hairs" with scissors. They were no longer afraid of the people who sheared their bell-bottom pants as symbols of the depraved West. Female students unveiling their faces no longer feared being attacked by fanatics who burned and mutilated women's faces with acid, claiming to be acting on behalf of the Koran and morality. Some female school principals encountered this misfortune in 1972—the year 1392 of the Islamic Hegira.

Today with the resurgence of religious fanaticism in the region, one can only hope that the zealots won't reemerge. And if they do, *137* that some educated women desperately seeking an identity with integrity, won't let themselves be taken in by the rhetoric. Elsewhere, I met women who in their search for identity fell into the trap of the veil of politics, the veil of provocation-to-the-depraved-West. Later, they came to realize that this veil had become a prison.

At first glance Yemen doesn't appear to reflect more than surface changes for women. To abandon the screen which protects a woman from the world, she has to be brave. In the streets of Sanaa you pass by multicolored "walking tents" or brush against flocks of "black birds." Under this hot, heavy, opaque disguise, girls, women and elders walk, laugh, talk with one another.

The colorful fabric of the "walking tents" is imported from Pakistan. It consists of a large piece of material with red, green and blue designs. A woman wraps it loosely around her body. It covers everything except her face which is hidden behind a piece of Yemenite cotton batik attached to her broad headband. She raises and lowers this batik like a curtain, depending on the circumstances. The batik's large, round red and white spots set on a black background make the woman look like a ghoul, staring at you from the night with blood-streaked eyes.

In the cities however, black attire prevails, an elegant black which can be worn anywhere. This austere screen goes over clothes. It's taken off when a woman is sheltered from men's eyes, either within the four walls of her home or inside a friend's house when only women are present. A long black skirt over her clothes is often held up by a leather belt. A black cape, tightly buttoned at the neck, covers the arms down to the wrist and goes down to the waist. A black scarf bandaged around her head—tied at the nape of the neck—only allows her eyes to show. Last, the woman puts on "the curtain" veil, which is also black, cinching it under the bandage of her black scarf. And of course under all this gear she wears her regular clothes; in the city, these are often the latest fashions from the West.

A Symbol

Veil or no veil: that is the question. But the question isn't simple. The veil symbolizes femininity. A veil is the perfect gift for a four year old girl on special occasions. Pretty ten year olds parading themselves in their new veils remind you of their little Western sisters who proudly display a perfectly useless bra on a perfectly flat chest. And so what if the oversized wings are heavy, drag in the dust and make you trip! An elegant veil can also be a sign of wealth. As soon as a poor man makes some money he hurries off to buy his wife a prison of fine cotton or silk.

The veil hides a woman's face and her shape but not her voice and the way she carries herself or walks. In the streets the woman behind the ghost can be recognized by dozens of little details by her husband, parents, girlfriends, or the young man who's engaged to her—or who dreams of being engaged to her.

Some just focus on one detail, however. I remember talking about this to an Egyptian gym teacher who teaches Sanaa's teenage girls. Her students were lined up in rows in the school courtyard doing calisthenics. Some had their veils on!

"How do you tell them apart?"

"I just look at the shape and colour of their shoes."

Eating or drinking in public is yet another calisthenic for a veiled woman. She has to turn away furtively, quickly flip back her veil-curtain, pull down her veil-bandage to uncover her mouth and then she can hastily gulp down her drink, her eyes always kept on the lookout. Sometimes she is in such a hurry that she accidently scalds her face with a hot drink.

But these acrobatics aren't everyday. They're only necessary when a woman is traveling from one city or village to another, when she stops on the street to eat or drink at a stand. Restaurants are reserved for men only, from the customers to the waiters, all the way down to the cook. The warm, matronly waitress doesn't exist in Yemen.

Women have meals with their families or among girlfriends, hidden from men's sight even if these men are their fathers,' brothers,' or husbands' friends. When a man comes home with guests he signals his arrival before entering the house by calling out the name of "Allah" several times long and loud enough so that the women have time to hide.

At the University of Sanaa, established in 1970, a canteen is reserved for female students—a little, discrete, well-protected room. The male student cafeteria, on the other hand, is large and wide open. The young women eat among themselves, unhampered by their masks, their veils and their fears. The most daring of them attend classes with their faces exposed; but many still fear losing their honor by leaving the cocoon and security of their closed world. Not a single girl, veiled or unveiled, will risk approaching male students.

Hide Your Face from the Devil

The problem of a meal eaten with or without the veil, with or without boys, is just one strand in the inextricable web of forbiddens forced upon the life of female students. A girl's reputation comes first; so where does she sleep when there's no more space in the girls' dormitories and God has made her a girl from outside the capital with no family connections in Sanaa?

Another obstacle to female freedom is the driver's license. To get one you have to have a picture taken. And to be photographed when you're a woman living in Sanaa, you have to take off the veil and show your face. In Arabic the photo negative is called "afrita", the devil. This devil must never see a woman's face, she has to hide it from him at all costs. What a tragedy if the negative-devil managed to capture female features in his blackness and later exposed them to the light—and to men's eyes!

A few young women, though, had the courage to say "To hell with Satan!" They broke the vicious circle, showing their faces and taking the steering wheel and the road to freedom. Others from stricter families are content to drive in secret, far away from the cities, chaperoned by their lord father, husband, or brother.

Getting a picture taken is definitely a dilemma for a Yemenite woman. The photographer who sets up shop and takes the snapshot is a man. The lab developing technician is also a man. And of course, both are forbidden to see a female smile. One of the more popular programs broadcast in the 80's by Radio-Sanaa was entitled: "The Solution to the Problem". A listener, preoccupied with this question asked,

"Isn't there a woman-photographer in Yemen or elsewhere who could open a studio just for women?"

During a visit to Sanaa a woman friend suggested that I apply for the job. But I obviously wasn't "the solution to the problem" and I still don't know if later any woman came to embody "the solution."

At the time, a Yemenite man, before going on a long trip across the country with one or more women from his family, had to go to the Ministry of the Interior in Sanaa. There he had to sign a paper certifying that the female bundles traveling with him were actually his wife, mother, sister or daughter. He then got the passes which were necessary to cross the checkpoints set at city entrances. These precautions were essential to national security. Under the veil you can see without being seen, you can spy, run-away, hide weapons
... or even carry off a woman out of love, or for the love of money.

Taxi drivers are strictly forbidden from driving a woman alone. This has even been broadcast by radio. Yet taxi drivers are allowed to pick up a bouquet of female customers and drive them all together. But only within city limits. On intercity roads female passengers must be accompanied by a male relative. A dozen women in a taxi aren't worth one man.

Modern But Respectable

One morning a Yemenite journalist relays an invitation to me from his young wife. The next day, early afternoon, he comes to pick me up at the hotel in his car. While I have the audacity to seat myself on the front seat next to him, he has the audacity to unleash a tape of Beatles music full-blast. We drive towards his house where a woman-only party awaits me. In front of the mosque we pull over and load two black packages from which four hands and four feet emerge. While the indiscernibles make themselves comfortable on the backseat, I ask my colleague,
"Who are they?"
"I don't know exactly who they are, they're friends of my wife. She wanted to invite them with you and told me to pick them up in front of the mosque."
I don't speak Arabic well enough to be able to make conversation with the two other female passengers and suggest to my chauffeur that he act as an interpreter.
"That's impossible. It just isn't done."
He smiles, looking a little embarrassed.
"It's disrespectful for a man to ask a woman her name."
Whether these women are single or married, young or old, I won't know until later.
"Do you often drive women you don't know?"
"Of course! Here we're always with women we don't know."
"But you do know your wife, don't you?"
He laughs.
"My wife is modern. She's fifteen years old and still goes to school. Outside the classroom she would never speak to one of her male professors. My wife never talks with a man who's a stranger to the family. She's modern but she knows how to behave."
After winding through dusty roads full of rocks, our driver drops us off at his door, my two companions still tucked under their black wings.

The Bird and the Veil

"Come here my little one, Feast will soon be here.
Take this veil, don't be scared. The veil is the dress
    of happiness."
This is how he spoke to my sister, a little flower of
    tender years
    still wet with the milk of the cradle.

And yet at age six how could she arouse desire or
    set hearts aflame!

She ran to me, stumbling over the folds of her long
    veils.
    a little bird with shackled wings, suddenly seized
    with fear.
I made myself laugh but how could I forget
the time when she could still show her sweet beauty.

While your yesterday was gentle and soft, mine also
    had the taste of fine fruit . . .
The flowers of our youth withered beneath the
    shadow of our veils.
We no longer spread the scent of lilies to starry
    skies . . .
Facing the sun, our eyes will never again mirror
    childrens' pure joy.

But that's the way it is.
We are women and for us everything is over
before we have even begun to live.

Mohamed al-Sharafi

(This Yemeni poem was translated from the French by Corinne Borel
and Laurence Deonna).

The house is new, but built in Yemen's traditional style. In spite of the high cost of working stone, brick laying and embellishing with stucco and stained glass, Yemenite architects are less likely to resort to standard ugly concrete.

The car drives off. Today, the master of the house can't even set foot at the door of his own home. What a scandal if he were to see the tip of the tip of one of the female guests' noses! But actually he could care less. I sensed his nervousness; he was anxious to get to the men's quat party which he wouldn't miss for anything.

A Gathering of Princesses

I hear steps and laughter. A hand grabs me, pulls me into the darkness of the narrow corridor. I enter, followed by my two mysterious ones who uncover their faces as soon as the door is closed. They look at me, burst out laughing, then peel off the layers of their veils. Their black capes and skirts join the heap thrown against the wall by the women who've arrived earlier.

As for myself, I just have my sandals to throw off.

Najjat, my fifteen year old hostess, is an adolescent with a child's smile. Her black mane hangs over an irridescent brocade dress, the color of the moon. I ask her if I can have a tour of the house.

It's a comfortable house with running water, a bathroom and a fully equipped kitchen. Daffy Duck stickers quack and dance on the kitchen wall. Elsewhere in Yemen, real poultry gobbles and clucks on the floors of old kitchens which are smoky caves set on the second story of towering labyrinth-like houses. They are suffocating, made with only one tiny hole in the wall for a window, "to protect women from drafts and indiscreet glances." The fowl share these kitchens with a stone oven, pitchers, jugs, dishes, pots and the women.

At Najjat's the room next to the kitchen is full of over-sized, cheap, showy Western couches. Though in the living room reserved for women, I rediscover the simple beauty of traditional Yemenite homes. The guests are astounding. The black ghosts of the streets have shed their shrouds and become dragonflies, flowers and princesses. Their dresses glitter and shimmer with cloth in all colors. They are apple-green, shocking pink, electric blue, golden yellow and threaded silver. Headbands and ribbons are wrapped around their heads. Heavy jewelry hangs around their necks. Their wrists glimmer with bracelets, their fingers are loaded down with rings. In a blend of perfumes I recognize Parisian Fidji and Miss Dior.

The women are elaborately made up. What a waste of seduction! Not a single man to succumb to it (they're all off chewing quat).

Sitting shoulder to shoulder against three of the white walls, the women's silhouettes form a long colorful ribbon which undulates as they move.

My arrival silences the surprised gathering. Voices die down, eyes stare at me. A hand finally signals me to sit down. Narrow thin mattresses carpet the edges of the room and lean against the lower walls. Here and there, multicolored pillows serve as seats or elbow cushions. Cardamom tea and a concoction of coffee husks are served in tiny porcelain cups, creating white splotches by the guests' feet. Large water pipes gurgle in the middle of the room, like a fountain gurgling peacefully in the middle of an old courtyard. The women's smoking ritual unravels like the men's.

Women Also Chew

Like the men, women chew quat, but in smaller amounts and not as often. Are they saving their money? No. Most likely they simply have less than the men, since in Yemen like everywhere else, men are the ones who have their pockets stuffed with the bills. Do women chew less out of vanity? Indeed, a snow-white set of teeth is more attractive than a mossy smile. Do they chew less for health reasons? It's known that the drug diminishes appetite and that an undernourished pregnant woman puts her baby at risk. Yet I've been told that as long as the future mother continues to eat normally, quat won't have obvious effects on her baby.

Women's quatmania varies from region to region. City women chew the cud more than peasant women. The mountain women of Djebel Sabr live off of it. You can see them tearing down the slopes with their baggy style pants ballooning out and their necklaces glinting in the sun; they're in a hurry to get to the Taiz market where they'll unwrap their precious green bundles. These wild, unveiled beauties look at you with daring eyes, they don't mince words and are tough business women. Their families' well being depends on their shrewd ability to lure and draw in customers. While they're busy unloading the quat, laying it out for display, calling out to customers and keeping track of their money, their men sit in the village resting. They're saving their strength for the afternoon quat party.

In Sanaa, at the woman's quat party, my young host Najjat looks distraught. I think she's worried that I don't like the local specialties. She suddenly disappears reappearing with a large tray, presenting me with an English teapot and a mug. Red and yellow Lipton tags hang out of the teapot which still has a price tag stuck to it. I'm touched by her solicitude. And these women are so nice. The youngest are amused by my presence. The oldest get up to come sit near me, putting an arm around my shoulder, touching my hair. They sniff at my perfume. They scrutinize my clothes, feeling them, gauging their quality and price, commenting on them. Their curiosity is insatiable. When they smile they show teeth turned green from quat. They're ageless.

Doubts

Everything seems so carefree and bathed in such peaceful contentment that I wonder if I've made a mistake in thinking that these women aren't happy. From my first trip to Yemen, I revolted against the life imposed on them. It hurt to see all the taboos paralyzing them. I've denounced their confinement, forced marriages, endless childbearing and the way their husbands impose divorce on them, leaving them no recourse. Yes, they go to school, sometimes they even go to the University or work in offices, but they're still kept on the fringes.

Yet today they're in front of me, laughing, teasing each other, giggling and chattering away. Are they really so happy? Is this a dream or are they keeping their secret well? Which is the truth? So many times I've seen sadness filling women's eyes here, their smiles smothered by resignation.

I remember a student who had just married. I asked her if she had ever dreamed of marrying a foreigner for love. She looked at me stupefied:

"What a strange idea! We don't even choose our Yemenite husbands!"

While traveling through Yemen I also wanted to find out what the men thought. I asked open-minded fathers if they would accept their daughters marrying a foreigner. Many replied that they would approve. Some even added,

"Life is very hard here for women."

Back in the women's living room, I relax in the warm atmosphere. Then I remember other faces, the sad taut faces which haunt our Western cities. Again I see our women workers rushing from their homes to the office, from the office to the supermarket and from the supermarket to their homes, utterly exhausted; our bored rich housewives sitting expressionless and silent in the buses; our lonely women, alone in a coffee house in front of a mountain of whipped cream; our aged women put away in retirement homes. Where is happiness then? Where is life harder?

The Catastrophe!

The afternoon comes to an end. The time will soon come when the guests put their veils back on and go home. A decent woman can't be out on the street after sundown.

But before the black birds fly off, two girls turn on a tape and dance. Their clear faces become dreamy dancing to the Eastern music. They ripple, their steps slide, their bodies undulate, yet their torsos are almost still and there is a faraway look in their eyes.

It's the picture that every journalist dreams of. Looking at the red and blue light coming through the stained glass window I ask myself if I need a flash. I reach over for my bag and pull out my camera . . .

The women react immediately. A grenade wouldn't have scared them more. Some jump up and run away covering their faces with their hands. Others turn to the wall, shielding themselves with their arms.

All through this catastrophe Najjat is an impeccable hostess. She rushes towards me, grabbing the camera with one hand and giving a gesture of disapproval with the other. I feel terrible. But I must confess that I knew it was risky. A picture of a woman in a newspaper or magazine is a scandal. Because of this picture the entire family may be dishonored.

During a wedding I once managed to snag a picture of some female guests. The next day the fifteen year old girl who had introduced me to my "victims" came to see me.

"My friends are panicked. Their husbands are absolutely furious and have ordered you to give them back the film."

Another time, a situation arose with a young woman returning from America where she had studied at the University of California, Berkeley. She gave me permission to take pictures of her. Later, when I returned to Europe I received a desperate letter. The mailman woke me at 7 AM, handing me a registered express letter. It said: "My father has found a husband for me. I'm going to get married. I beg of you, *please* don't publish my photograph in your book."

"Dance!"

Najjat's friends have gone back to their seats. I shyly try to smile, asking them forgiveness, but they don't smile back. I feel more and more uneasy. Unable to look at them I stare at my bare feet.

Suddenly, I hear a voice calling me:

"Ya souhoufiya! Hey you, journalist!"

A young woman beckons me over to her. She holds up the tape player:

"Ouroussi! Dance!"

Putting the machine back down she puts on a tape. I flashback to childhood when if you lost the game you had to pay with a chocolate, a kiss, or do something ridiculous.

Allright girls, I lost. I have to pay.

And I pay. To a tune from 1925! The Charleston! The warped sound of the tape sings, "Yes sir, that's my baby!" What a ball! "Yes sir," I get into the mood. "Yes sir," I put my sandals back on. "Yes sir," I slide along. "Yes sir!" I hike up my skirt, roll it up my belt. "Yes sir," I borrow a headband. "Yes sir!" I borrow a necklace. "Yes sir!" I swing my hips. "Yes sir!" I go wild!

The women sway to the music and clap their hands madly. "Yes sir," journalism can lead to anything. Even to Charlestoning as punishment to entertain the harems of Yemen.

It's true that here entertainment is rare for women. The movie theatre is male turf, a noisy place thick with laughter and greasy paper wrappings. In Sanaa, women are not allowed to enter the movie theatre except on the Friday sabbath at a showing reserved "for women and families."

Since video has become popular women prefer to see movies at home. "Bonnie and Clyde" and "Funny Girl" have replaced the traditional women balladeers and entertainers, the Djemilas and Aichas of former celebrations. These traditional entertainers used to perform for visitors coming to see a new mother who was enjoying the traditional forty days of postpartum rest. According to custom the mother leaves her bedroom mattress for a high bed where she receives her guests. Women relatives, girlfriends and neighbors come to the bedside of the forty day queen to pay their respects and wish her well.

Weddings

But the biggest entertainment for women, even more so than movies or religious holidays, is weddings. Somebody else's wedding of course, getting married isn't always fun. In Yemen, the festivities vary little from region to region. The celebration lasts three days with the ritual of visits and banquets, guttural traditional chants, pulsing drums and tamborines, stamping warrior dances, women's shrill ululating and the honking of horns drowned out by explosions of gunshots.

Except in some rural villages, women and men are never together during weddings.

It was in Sanaa on a very clear night. In spite of the rich milky way of stars in the sky, my eyes were on the garland of lights strung between the street and the bride's house in a myriad of colors. Not far from the front door, a human garland was unwinding its black drapes and rainbow of fabrics. These women were ululating, standing on a low wall, the silhouette of their veils against the sky. Some smiled at me. *Their photograph is on the cover of this book.*

I enter the house, then go through the low door to the harem's room, the "afrita" devil hanging on my shoulder—my camera. At the sight of this apparition the aviary of women goes silent. The glare of the bride and her beautifully adorned birds resign me to abandoning Satan, so I tuck him under a mattress.

But I still have the eyes that God gave me!

The bride overlooks the gathering perched on top of a pile of pillows. She is from a modern wealthy city family and isn't the traditional over-adorned statue. Customarily the bride is crowned with a huge, cone-like tiara covered with gems and fresh flowers. With this heavy load she's also weighed down by masses of jewelry (some of which may be borrowed). But here I find a Western mannequin, thick with ruffles and organdy frills, wearing nylon gloves and vinyl shoes. She's decorated with gold so thin it looks fake. The heroine of the day has bartered her Yemenite attire for a white imported wedding dress from the West.

Clothes are changed easier than customs, however, and old marriage rites are still very much alive in Yemen. On the first day, after the future wife is bathed, the palms of her hands and soles of her feet are dyed with henna. The second day the "musayena"—the "woman decorator"—draws fine black designs on her hands, arms, breasts, sometimes her whole body—the location depending on regional customs. Those who want to dress up with the bride have themselves decorated too. Her friends bathe her in gifts. Her fiance gives her the traditional chest or a modern suitcase containing dresses and jewels, the quality and quantity of which depend on his wealth. The girl is then displayed, sitting silent and still. All around her bouquets of aromatic herbs are laid. With them are plates where burning candles and eggs are set to symbolize lon- *149* gevity and especially fertility—without fertility a woman has little reason to exist.

The third day the family shrine, a spectacularly adorned princess covered with veils, is escorted by her father and uncle to her husband's home. She's awaited by the women of her in-laws' family who will give her the traditional intimate examination verifying her virginity. The very young bride trembles.

The future husband trembles too. He's never seen his future wife without her veil; he doesn't really know if she's ugly or beautiful. Except if his in-laws are modern enough to have secretly slid a Polaroid photo of her into his hand—or if she's a cousin who he's had a glance of as a child. He also has other fears; the verdict from the women in his family. In Yemen a young flower which has already been landed on by a butterfly loses all value; you can divorce her on the spot.

But there are ways to make arrangements with the powers on high—with much female solidarity. Women know all the tricks and ingenious devices to make a flower young and budding again. Later the flower might even have a good laugh with her friends. I've been at a women's gathering where a fourteen year old girl, just married, ruthlessly mimicked her aged husband's weaknesses.

The Candles and the Groom

Another night just as clear, I was drawn by other matrimonial garlands. It was in a small town north of Sanaa. This time the necklace of lights led me to a solid looking house; the house of the Sheikh. Weddings and political gatherings for the community are usually held in his halls.

That evening I once again found myself the only woman in a world of men.

Going through the large wide-open door I almost stumbled over a group of ten year old boys, busy around an old-fashioned black wood stove. Their task was to keep the water pipes going. Tending to the fire in the stove, they would pick up red hot coals and rush upstairs to feed the pipes. They ran up and down all night long.

The groom entertained his friends on the second floor. There must have been a hundred of them slumped against the walls, numbed by quat, simmering in a thick cloud of smoke. The water pipes burned incessantly. The air was suffocating. Surrounded by hazy silhouettes I walked through a cloudy dream, feeling layers of quat leaves under my bare feet.

Such a picture is not common in Yemen. You'll hardly see any in the photographers' shop-windows. A woman must not show her face in public. For family pictures the father usually poses alone with the children.

A limp arm beckoned me to sit down, a swollen cheek attempted a vague smile, but I only wanted one thing: to get out of there! These men's crazy nights sometimes last until morning . . . and to think that they had already spent the whole day dancing and shooting, holding up their daggers and guns!

Deciding to leave this smoky men's world, I glided off into the night.

Just as the bride has her three days of celebration, so does the groom. The third day of the wedding, after having bathed, he goes to the mosque, still flanked by his ever-present cohorts. One night I came across one of these processions. The future husband was leaning on two friends. He looked like a sad prophet with a long grey scarf draped over his turban, hanging at either side of his face. Other friends held out trays covered with lit candles. A little boy proudly displayed a Libby's can filled with a bouquet of aromatic herbs and topped with a candle. The group made its way through the alley with kerosene lanterns flickering their flames into the night.

The men sang along with music. It came out of a loudspeaker whose size and shape reminded me of the horn on a gramophone I had seen on old records. On the picture, a RCA-like dog was cocking its ear to "His Master's Voice"—the name of the record label. Here in Yemen, a boy scurried along to keep up with the man holding the loudspeaker; it had been plugged into the cassette player which the little one cautiously held in his hands.

Rallied by his friends and their songs, the future husband finally reached his house. His companions left him alone to wait for his fiancee. She finally arrived. This would be the house where she would spend her days constantly surrounded by her in-laws. From then on, like all proper women, she would be listening closely for the slightest variation in "her master's voice."

The Little Brides

Plans have been made in Sanaa for legal measures to forbid the marriage of girls under sixteen. Will this law ever be ratified? And if it is, will it ever be enforced? Girls are often married having barely reached puberty. But when a good deal can be made between two families three year old girls are legally engaged, their futures decided permanently. Until the day she's married the promised little one will usually continue to live with her parents. If her family is very poor, the baby bride is sometimes given away earlier to in-laws; while waiting to play the role of a wife, she'll play the role of a servant. The Yemenite woman rarely marries the man of her dreams. Her father's choice is sometimes a man his age or even his own father's age. Polygamy still exists in Yemen, especially in the rural areas.

Getting A Good Deal

Leila is a secretary in a ministry of Sanaa. Through the slit of her cloth mask, her eyes watch her work while her hands move quickly on the IBM typewriter. When she sees me her hands freeze. She turns towards me. From the sudden folding of the veil around her mouth I deduce that Leila is smiling at me.

"I'm lucky," she says. "When my husband saw my face unveiled for the first time he thought I was beautiful. He's good for me. They married me at fifteen. Now I'm nineteen with two children, two girls."

"How did you get to know each other?"

"A neighbor introduced us with the consent of our families. I liked him. I said 'yes.' Our engagement lasted seven months. We even went to the movies alone . . ."

"That whole time you were still wearing your veil? You never slid it down just a bit . . . not even a little bit?"

"Never."

"And what about your daughters?"

"I hope they won't have to wear the veil. I hope they'll be able to choose their husbands instead of being sold like sheep."

A high official in Sanaa once bluntly said to me,

"Here marriage isn't a market, it's a racket!"

In this country where virility is boasted . . . patriarchs are thrilled at the birth of a baby girl. In northern Yemen a woman, virgin and beautiful, is worth her weight in rials. I met a man planning to get married. He was overwhelmed.

"My future father-in-law is demanding 200,000 rials for his daughter. And even that isn't enough. Now he wants the keys to a Mercedes."

A daughter's divorce isn't a disaster for the shrewd father. If he's business minded he may even move things along. A divorcee can be remarried. Her price will be reduced of course, but for a real businessman no profit is too small!

I remember Djemila. She had lost her father and her brother Ahmed had become the head of the family. He was adamant that his sister be married. A very rich old man made an offer. This unprecedented offer fell out of his toothless mouth and Djemila, backed by her mother, refused. Her brother Ahmed paid a visit to the rejected old man. The love for his sister and his love of money were confused in his heart. He said to the suitor,

"If I want to I can force her to marry you. But if she leaves you in a few days don't come complaining. In any case, my friend, don't count on me to give you a refund."

Some husbands try to recover the money they've invested in a conjugal venture, which is often a small fortune. Young women who've studied or have had training are in demand. They can sell their skills and with their salaries slowly pay back their husbands' capital outlay.

A Revolutionary Law?

In 1976, in an attempt to discourage the marriage business and reduce the cost of weddings, the Sanaa government declared a law setting the price for a wife at 165 rials—no more (traditionally a widow or a divorcee is half-price).

According to custom the happy husband of a virgin has to pay directly to his wife the "morning right," also called "right of entry." The new law limits this gift to only 50 rials.

As for the wedding festivities, only a simple tea-party is allowed. Good-bye quat, roasted lambs, processions in cars and shooting guns! It's no picnic for those who decide to go beyond the authorized debaucheries; they have to pay high fines which are used to finance the cooperatives.

A man who plans to take a second wife—usually under the pretext that the first one is sterile—has to pay out 1000 rials. He has the choice to give this money to his first wife or to the State treasury for cooperatives.

The head of a family can demand up to 20,000 rials from a foreigner who wants to marry his daughter. But he can only keep the 165 rials allowed by law. The cooperatives pocket the rest.

In you dissect all these articles in the new Sanaa marriage law you can discern that women, with their feminine charms and their monetary value, contribute to financing Yemen's development. They no longer just offer the fruits of their wombs, but also telephone poles, water pipes, and roads; the birth of a new country. Their wombs have been transformed into factories, the slaves of Tradition have become the slaves of the Revolution.

If the law were applied, men would have less reason to go work
in rich countries in the hopes of making enough money for mar-

In Taiz, at the Indochina and Suez Bank, these two office girls don't wear the veil. One comes from Somalia, the other from Djibouti.

Two mysteries: the veil and the computer (Central Postal Administration, Sanaa).

riage. But in fact the law satisfies only the lawmakers and the value of a wife keeps going up at the Sanaa Stock Exchange. People continue to spend and make money on marriage and the cooperatives just try to get by.

Marriage arrangements can become a family obsession. I closely followed the dexterity of a father faced with all the problematic developments in a marriage transaction.

"You see," he explained. "If I obey the law and the other one doesn't, I lose. I have a son and a daughter. Let's say I give away my daughter for 165 rials like the law says, O.K. Then afterwards what am I supposed to do if I want to hitch up my son? I may need thousands of rials to marry him since his future in-laws could well be greedier than the law."

The marriage arabesque Yemenite style is difficult for a Western mind to grasp. As fate had it, I again found myself indiscreetly in an all-male meeting, trying to follow the complicated steps to marriage. Two heads of families were fiercely debating the future of their progeny.

"O.K., my daughter's divorced, you can have her for 50,000 rials, but what about me? I have to find a young wife for my son. It costs big bucks! . . . Allright . . . I'll give you a special price, but what are you going to do for me? When it's my turn are you going to help me come up with the extra money I'll need for my son's wife?"

Many wondered why some young men from North Yemen kept peeking over to South Yemen. It wasn't a question of fascination with an ideology. They hadn't acquired a sudden taste for communism. It was simply that in Aden this crazy marriage market had been made illegal.

And what now that the two Yemens have united? Rumor has it that some men from the South rushed to the North to buy themselves a second wife . . . while at the same time, unveiled and wearing colorful dresses, women demonstrated in Aden their refusal to be bundled up in black veils like their sisters in the North. Where will the wind of History blow? Only time will tell.

Love, School and Freedom

Minds don't change with the touch of a magic wand. Yet the Revolution fairy has moderated Yemenite's mores and made them more
merciful to the inclinations of romance.

The red rose of love doesn't grow easily on Islamic soil. It used to be that in Yemen, whoever picked it out of wedlock risked a hundred whip lashings, if single, and was put to death by stoning or sword, if married. Before the execution, the guilty couple was paraded in the streets for an entire day with a drum strapped to their backs—the drummer would pound on it full force to alert the people.

The professionals of "morality watch" alerted by neighbors' gossip, would barge in on lovers, then report them. I've been told that there were three of them in Sanaa designated by the Iman himself. But this miserable profession went to meet its Maker; the Revolution swept away the executors by executing them. It is said that one of them escaped because he had connections in high places.

Today in most parts of Yemen an unfaithful wife "only" gets a few weeks in prison; the majority of women prisoners are adulteresses. Adultery committed by women is still "unforgiveable", while adultery committed by a man always has a good excuse; he can easily make some kind of a deal.

While prisons still close in on women who dream of love, schools open their doors for illiterate women who dream of knowledge. There are thousands of these women who seek to learn. Like Anissa in Taiz, who twice a week escapes the house to rush to the Women's Association school, forgetting the kids, the pots and the pans. The place could be called "Women's Happiness." Here you study, type, knit, sew and make frills. Here you indulge in socializing with peace of mind knowing that your reputation is protected. Education sanctions your activities as religion does under other circumstances.

But much more than the chit chat, the women discover freedom. Above all the freedom to write. The freedom to be able to write for themselves without having to ask somebody. Among these women there are many emigrants' wives who, after years, are finally free to communicate directly with their husbands.

Anissa, whose face is round like a full moon, is a dedicated student. I go sit on the bench next to her. Looking like a nun under the black and white of her veil, her luminous smile reflects a warm heart and makes the gold in her teeth shine—the gold stars in her mouth aren't just to enhance her beauty, they're capital.

"I'm thirty-five," Anissa tells me. "When we were kids, girls didn't go to school."

How can one become enlightened with knowledge under an unenlightened despot? Under the Imam's rule even the boys were   *157*

Early morning in Hodeyda on the Red Sea. This little girl's elder sister was married the night before and the child asked to have her hands decorated with henna just like her.

Djebel Sabr mountain, above the city of Taiz. While the young women ran away from the camera, the old lady smiled. She feared no more for her reputation; age gave her not only authority but also freedom.

barely educated. In the hard times after the Revolution, when education had just started, people took turns offering their homes as classrooms or the lessons were taught at the mosque. Even today, in nearly inaccessible villages at the end of roads, classes are still held under the shade of a tree. The teachers—Egyptian, Sudanese and Yemenite—manage with what they've got.

However, real school buildings are now popping up everywhere in Yemen. In the North it's often Saudi Arabia which has paid for the construction, furniture, teachers' salaries and books. In this region the majority of primary school texts come from Arabia. By printing books the rich Saudian fairy godmother hopes to make an imprint on minds. Through her generosity to her Yemenite godson she locks him behind the rigid doors of Islam—other countries though, provide generous aid without requiring that the building of a school be linked to the building of a mosque.

In Yemen males have priority in access to education more than in other places. Yet, in city schools the number of girls is increasing. But I've been told that in villages, the average ratio remains one girl for every ten boys. Unfortunately most of these girls leave school before adolescence to get married . . . and are sometimes divorced by their husbands shortly after.

"Only My Jewelry and My Soul Belong to Me"

I met a school inspector from Zebid—once Yemen's city of high culture. This modern scholar welcomed his journalist guest while lying on a bed and leaning on an elbow, just like a Roman. The bed was a high platform, 3 feet off the ground with a woven rope seat. All around the scholar's books, manuscripts and parchments spilled out of the small closets and niches built into the white walls. Outside in the alley, the hot humid air was stifling. Inside the house, coolness emanated from the frequently watered beaten earth (water is also used to keep away insects).

"In ancient times in Zebid," the scholar began, "mosques with a medresa—a school—were given female names, even though only boys were allowed. Fortunately everything has changed, today a third of the city's women sit on the benches of knowledge."

The women of Zebid can sit on the benches of knowledge but they can't cross the walls to freedom. The wall enclosure of their schoolyard has been raised 10 feet by the city council. Veiled in the streets and prisoners in school, they live like cloistered nuns. What a scandal if a man were to plunge his gaze into the schoolyard from a nearby window and discern a female form!

City of Taiz. For many wives and mothers, the schools put up by the Union of Women (a governmental organization) mean freedom. Here you can indulge in socializing with peace of mind knowing that your reputation is protected.

Right: In a school near Saada, in the far north.

Below: In the village schools the ratio was one girl for every ten boys. Now the number of girls is slowly increasing.

But what needs to change isn't only the way men look at women, but the way women look at themselves (and not only in Yemen!). In Sanaa the Yemenite Women's Association, with the support of the Ministries of Education and Social Affairs and radio and TV, encourages women to take off their veils . . . and unveil their true personalities. One of the Association's representatives denounced certain restrictive laws:

"A man can repudiate his wife under any pretext but the wife who wants a divorce has to go to Islamic court. And all this is with the benediction of our so-called egalitarian Constitution . . . which in turn is based on Islamic law. . . . We'll also have to stop being bought and sold."

In Taiz at one of the Women's Association classes, most of the students are mothers. I ask them,

"What more than anything in the world do you want for your daughter?"

Anissa closes her eyes. I sense that she desperately wants to express the feeling of millions of silenced women.

"I pray that she'll marry a man she loves. . . ."

I finish her sentence with the standard cliché,

". . . and that she'll live happily ever after and have many children."

"Oh no! Three is enough!"

The students' veils rustle as they turn in their seats to talk to each other. A voice suddenly emerges from the brouhaha,

"Anissa is right! Three kids are plenty!"

The protest has burst out through a red poppy-colored veil:

"I have three children. The youngest is two years old. I've managed to stop there but my husband's furious. He's dragged me to the doctor . . . he's threatening to divorce me."

The classroom suddenly goes silent. Looking around me I see sadness clouding over the few uncovered faces, I can sense the gloom under the veils. The red mask has denounced the truth: a woman is not master of her body. A nomadic woman once told me: "Only my jewelry and my soul belong to me."

Ruffling the Feathers Of Tradition

What use does the Yemen Family Planning Association have if the birth control it promotes can lead to repudiation—just as the red masked woman said? There must be open-minded husbands. Or sly women! This is what I wanted to find out as I pushed open the door of the Association's Sanaa office (others are located in Taiz, Hodeyda and other cities).

The Yemenite Family Planning Association was founded in 1976. Overseen by the Ministry of Health, backed by the Yemenite Women's Association, supported by the International Family Planning Movement, this "revolutionary" Association works so discreetly that few Yemenites even know it exists. Its director, a man spiced with peppery humor, confides in me,

"It's dangerous to pluck the feathers of tradition. For a Yemenite a child is the gift of Allah. To refuse a child is to offend Him."

How well I know what he's talking about since so many times I've heard the same claim beneath the ringing of church bells.

"We can't afford to advertise birth control aggressively. We have to be content with disseminating five short minutes of information on radio and family TV. Here and there we manage to squeeze in a few articles in the general press and we also have a monthly newsletter."

"No other problems?"

"In our society a woman won't show her body to a man and we have a shortage of women doctors here. Almost all our women doctors come from abroad. Don't forget that now is the very first time that Yemenite women have ever been allowed to study in medical school."

The Yemen Family Planning Association—though backed by the Yemenite organizations—has to work discreetly.

"And what about money?"

"We're poor. Very poor. Our medical staff already takes up half the annual budget ($50,000). You're going to laugh, since fuel is so expensive I've even gotten down on my knees in front of my car, begging it to walk!"

My director-comedian adds,

"Saudi Arabia, usually so generous to Yemen, hasn't given me any oil; the Saudis are against birth control."

"Is there a problem with overpopulation here?"

"No. But that's no reason to make women into brood hens. It's so sad seeing their tired faces. For lack of proper food and hygiene their children die like little chicks. Why not replace the so-called "natural" balance of mortality with the rational balance of contraception?"

"That's a fine dream," I say, "But will you be able to convince Yemenite men, the legislators and the women themselves, that the value of a wife doesn't depend on her ability to have a string of children?"

He interrupts my pessimism,

"Dear madam, people are changing. Even in the countryside. Not all women believe they'll be condemned to hell for using contraception. Not all men go on the warpath when our medical teams arrive. Actually, foreign medical teams are often the ones to distribute our contraceptives."

Before I leave, the director wants to add that in spite of the weight of tradition, he's often witnessed kindness and understanding by men for their women.

The Moon's Cycles

I myself was touched by the sight of a very old man struggling up a doctor's winding staircase, trying to carry a load even more fragile than himself: his sick and dying wife.

Nor will I forget the anxious husband with whom I shared a taxi in the company of his wife, my interpreter, two bearded travelers, a Kalachnikov machine gun, a bundle of quat, and three chickens.

After miles of being silent and still, the black veiled mass pressed up against me in the taxi came to life. A hand emerged from her veils and pulled out a loaf of sweet corn bread from a plastic bag, offering me a slice. Then the woman suddenly placed her hand on my stomach.

"No baby? And what about the other ones? Where did you leave your children?"

"I don't have any."

A woman without children! Under my neighbor's mask I imagine her utter pity for me.

Her husband butts in,

"Here in Yemen we have lots of kids. But some men go too far: their wives are exhausted."

He pauses, then turns to my interpreter whom he thinks is my husband:

"Does your wife eat the pills against babies? The German nurse gave some to mine. But since then my wife no longer follows the cycles of the moon and her belly and breasts are as swollen and hard as a water jug. I'm very worried about her."

Never in Europe have I heard a single man speaking to me this way on a bus!

Evil Eye and Good Pills

Another time I'm driving towards Taiz through the region's hills when a pyramid of turquoise blue nylon suddenly appears around a bend in the road, a modern nomad's tent blowing in the wind with a camel standing next to it.

I walk over to get a better look. Four adorned birds rush to meet me with a fluttering of satin wings. These bedouin women are so short and small that when I saw them from a distance I thought they were children. They have bouquets of aromatic herbs tucked into their turbans, necks and chests laden with massive jewelry of all kinds and ears pierced with large rings decorated in silver beads. A tiny modern key hangs from a nylon string, dangling between the necklaces. It's the key to the big painted metal trunk where Yemenite women keep their clothes and paraphernalia.

These women belong to the lowest caste, the Khadams, who provide the servants, slaughterers, "hamam" keepers, street sweepers and outdoor barbers for Yemenite society. Khadams only marry among themselves. Most of them are semi-nomadic. Scattered around the edge of cities, their tents are usually dilapidated and patched, though sometimes equipped with T.V. antennas.

The Khadams like everyone in the country give generous hospitality. The women beckon me to the shade of their blue cloth walls, offering me the tea of friendship. They have the dark skin

and African features found among peasants on the Red Sea coast and among descendants of slaves. Slavery in Yemen was only yesterday . . .

One of the women suddenly lifts up her skirt, the second one follows and then the third. Do they think I'm a German or Swedish nurse because of my white blouse and light-colored eyes? All three of them show me their swollen hardened stomachs, obviously sick. In several places I see burn scars—cauterization is supposed to bring out the evil spirits of sickness.

Many here believe their illnesses are caused by djinns, the evil eye or a curse put on them by an enemy. Those with religious power, especially in the villages, do nothing to discourage these beliefs. Medical teams and representatives from the Yemenite Women's Association going out into the field, often find babies covered with amulettes but getting no medical care from their mothers.

Instead of going to the doctor, a mother asks the corner mosque sheikh to choose a verse from the Koran which he thinks is suited to her baby's illness. The sheikh then writes the verse on a piece of paper which is then swaddled up into a small cloth and hung on the baby's neck. Some families still drink from the silver "healing bowl" inscribed with sacred citations. There are thousands of men and women healers. The Yemenite buys medicinal herbs in the souk or picks them himself in the fields.

Back in the blue nylon tent with my three bedouin hostesses. The oldest one goes off into the darkest corner, kneels down to dig through her trunk, returns with a small bottle of pills and hands it to me. On the label I see the name of a Taiz hospital, instructions and the word "tuberculosis" in Arabic and English.

The youngest bedouin pulls at my sleeve. While looking over at the small vial of pills with a frown on her face she mimes pain, doubled over, clutching her stomach. She then shows me her cheek swollen with quat and lets out a sigh of bliss. Her message is clear:

"See, all these modern remedies are useless. Only quat relieves pain."

Pains

Of course the medicine is useless if you only take it when you're in the mood. Treating Yemen's most common illnesses—tuberculosis, chronic gastro-enteritis, bilharzia, malaria, amoebas, polio—is no easy task. Vaccination campaigns are underway. Cancer is rare and heart disease isn't common among the Yemenites who never stop struggling up mountains and climbing steep stairs.

Fatal complications for women during childbirth, on the other hand, are more common. They're often due to a lack of doctors and hospitals located close enough to their villages. Though abortion is illegal, this hasn't stopped women in North Yemen, as elsewhere, from risking their lives.

The clitoris is ruthlessly cut off women living in some regions of the Tihama plains bordering the Red Sea and Africa—an operation which is customary in many parts of Africa. The clitoridectomy is performed on little girls with no hygiene or anesthesia. (The Yemen Family Planning Association is against this dangerous practice.) Moreover, a circumcised woman will never know pleasure.

The Yemenite peasant woman suffers from back and muscular pains, not to mention bone deformations. She endlessly carries water jugs on her head and hauls huge loads of wood on her back, up to 100 pounds, for the kitchen oven. Often she's also depleted from intestinal parasites and anemia due to an unbalanced diet.

"The Dish's Daughter"

Sorghum and grains are Yemen's staple foods. For the poor, rice, beans, vegetables, eggs and cheese are small luxuries. The majority of women and children eat meager meals when they're alone. But as soon as the men return, especially if they have guests, meat and fruits reappear in abundance on the family mat. Men have first serve in both quality and quantity.

One night in Sanaa's old city, Bab-el-Yemen, a family unrolled its dinner mat for me. I sat on the ground placing my behind on a cushion, sniffing at the vapors steaming from the aluminum plates. I tore a piece of the "lahouh", a very thin bread and dipped it into the "zahawik", a reddish sauce made with tomatoes, carrots and garlic.

Around me each uses his bread to help himself to the "tabikh" made of ground meat, potatoes, onions and tomatoes. The little bowl and spoon set in front of me is for the "holba", a kind of green soup served at all Yemenite meals.

The "shafout" is another specialty. It's a mushy whitish kind of bread full of holes which make it look like a thick spiders web. Out of curiosity I have a bite, then hurry on to the salad, which is definitely tastier.

After the intoxication of the afternoon's quat party, my host, the master of the house, refreshes himself with a yogurt drink. His son sitting next to me does the honors to "the dish's daughter," the "bint el sahn" a cake made of flour, eggs, butter and honey.

His sister, a plump enough student, prefers to keep her fingers off it. She's a modern girl. Her mother though, still walled off by tradition, doesn't share our meal. From time to time the old woman leaves the kitchen downstairs to come peer at me from the door-way—it's a rare opportunity for her to see a woman foreigner. Excluded from the banquet that she herself has prepared, she gives me a smile from off in her corner, then returns to her duties.

A Militant

I've come across so many women in Yemen. I've seen their eyes.

To bring these stories of women's lives to a close, I would like to paint a portrait of a young woman who looks life straight in the face. When I met her she was the President of the Sanaa Women's Association.

Raufa Hassan is a journalist. Among other things, she was responsible for the feature page of "The Revolution" newspaper. Under the modest black scarf and the proper-looking velvet jacket, she looks fragile; but this is only an appearance. Raufa seems oblivious to conventions. She travels alone and writes and says what she thinks. Raufa even has her photo appear with her editorial column.

"I was educated in Cairo," she told me. "In Egypt I was already a rebel. One day a male student thinking he was funny, wrote on the University wall, 'A woman is like a pair of shoes, you can't do without them.' "

Still raging from that long ago insult she said to me,

"I grabbed the joker by the sleeve and told him, 'So your mother, your sister, your fiancée, are just a pair of shoes?' The idiot didn't apologize but the next day the graffiti was gone."

You can't pull the wool—or the veil—over Raufa's eyes!

She isn't alone. Many forget that throughout Yemen's history not all women have been eclipsed. The legendary kings of Yemen were . . . Women. When you ask a full-blooded Yemenite man who were Yemen's great kings, he'll answer,

"Uhh . . . Bilkis and Arwa."

Today these names—the names of the Queen of Sheeba and the Queen of Ibb from long ago—are still given to newborn baby girls of Yemen.

CHAPTER SIX

A Miracle of Radio on the Waves of Emigration

Me, a poor Yemenite with no oil, I worked almost my whole life under the scent of black gold!"

When I had met him some years ago, Farag, once an emigrant, was a taxi driver in Sanaa. Angrily gripping his vinyl wrapped steering wheel, he had continued:

"They say there's no oil in Yemen. I want to see it! They say they didn't find anything. Or not enough. Black gold bubbles up like a fountain of prosperity for our Saudi neighbors, so why not here where the land is the same? The truth is that a rich Yemenite wouldn't please anyone and a Yemenite laborer pleases everybody!"

The fine modern story read like a fable from olden times, traveling from person to person, running across the plains, penetrating the mountains, being enhanced all the time by yet new details. It said that oil was sleeping under Yemenite soil and that the Saudis, as the price for their generosity towards Yemen, demanded that Yemenites just be content with having dreams and selling the labor of their backs.

Now the story was not just a legend! Oil was found in Yemen and American companies have exploited it since 1985. The black gold was lying under the sands of the Arrub' el-Khālī desert, in the east, near Marib, the ancient capital of the Queen of Sheba. To each time its wealth, its myth, its grandeur . . .

But back to Farag's story:

"I was thirteen years old when I left for Mecca, dressed for the pilgrimage. I returned from the pilgrimage . . . twenty-five years later! I was a mason, a handyman, and fixed engines. In Arabia at prayer time they get indignant if you forget to close up shop. Some run after you with a stick."

"Did you send your salary to Yemen regularly?"

"Three or four times a year, and only through an emigrant visiting the village. He would give the money directly to my mother. This way it wouldn't disappear into my own brothers' pockets!"

Farag readjusts his turban, brushing it against the icicles of woolly pompoms which decorate the taxi's ceiling. The whole car is fringed and festooned. My chauffeur armed with a huge dagger, drives in a boudoir!

"I came back loaded with big money and driving my own taxi. I brought everything I owned with me when I left. I don't know of many emigrants who'll mail their money or wire it through a bank account."

The millions of dollars earned by Yemenites abroad continuously make their way back to Yemen. When a bank is founded stocks are first sold to former emigrants. Along with other advantages for the repatriated who want to go into business, the government grants land, tax exemptions and project feasibility studies performed by foreign firms for their planned enterprizes.

"The State does a lot," says Farag. "O.K.! But it isn't enough. The government should have better price controls. I came back because I love my country, but the cost of living in Yemen is really too high!"

"Are you married?"

"I wasn't able to offer myself the luxury of a wife for the twenty-five years I was away. I had to wait until I came back. She was divorced with no children so she cost me only 70,000 rials. My father-in-law gave her to me on credit. I've already paid 35.000 rials and I still pay 2,000 rials a month. Like many former emigrants I don't chew quat so I save a lot of money. I'm happy. I have my house, my taxi, and my wife who's expecting a baby. God be praised!"

The pompom taxi slows down, brakes, and comes to a halt. I've arrived. I open my bag, riffle through my wallet. I pull out some ragged bills, place them in the driver's hand and ask him, "And what about love in all this matrimonial wheeling and dealing?"

Farag picks his ear with his car key, then bursts out laughing. He puts a pensive finger on his forehead and confesses,

"Love is fine for the West, but Yemenites only care about money!"

In many villages, women, children and old people are left alone to cultivate the land. It is said that at least one third of the male population emigrated, not only to the oil rich neighboring Arab States but all over the world. Be it in times ancient or modern, the Yemenites always left by land or sea— and, nowadays, by air when they can.

Where They Speak of Vietnam

Yet, it is out of love that many "Yemenite-Vietnamese" families have been conceived. A peculiar tribe stuck in a refugee camp near Taiz since 1976, there are about 300 of them packed into concrete bungalows built around a large courtyard at the edge of the city. Even though all it would take would be to extend a line to the power cables running along the road, they have no electricity. Most of them are born of a Yemenite father and a Vietnamese mother. Some have kept Arab traits or have inherited high Asian cheekbones, others are veritable Vietnamese with smooth skin and eyes like button-holes, set in a round face. All are allegedly related by blood or marriage to the descendants of Yemenite sailors and merchants who at the beginning of the century left Aden bound for Asia. They settled there and opened businesses and restaurants.

Taken under the wing of their Imam, the Yemenite community of Vietnam consisted of 1200 people before the fall of Saigon in 1975. Many among them, linked by financial or professional interests to the French, then the Americans, quaked at the idea of a communist victory.

The War

Today the Imam of Saigon, Abdelrahman Ibn Hussein El-Khatibi, meets with me in Taiz. He is very dignified, sitting on a folding chair in the shadow of one of the refugee camp walls. He has lively eyes and his goatee and mustache are as immaculate as his scarf and turban. The patriarch, granddaddy of chubby-cheeked babies with slit eyes, presides over the destiny of the little Yemenite-Saigon community that's exiled . . . in Yemen!

To soothe his soul and those of his flock the Imam, barely arrived, asked that a mosque be built. The Saudis, grand providers of minarets, were solicited in vain. The site chosen by the "Vietnamese" was in their opinion, too discreet. It was only a piece of cheap land, quite far from the road; people passing wouldn't have been able to admire the beauty of the building and, especially, the generosity of Saudi Arabia. . .

"No mosque, but who cares since God is everywhere," the Imam resolves wisely.

It's wisdom and foresight which inspired him to act in 1975.

"Everything pointed to the communists taking over Saigon any day. I took the necessary precautions. I wrote to the Yemenite embassy in Beijing to ask for their help. In spite of all the years spent in Vietnam, we were still Yemenite citizens. I registered all the newborns in my big notebook."

The Imam, his scarf blowing in the wind, slips away for a moment. He reappears carrying a simple vinyl briefcase from which he pulls a letter, handing it to me like a relic.

"Here is a copy of the report I sent in 1975 to our Yemenite diplomats in China, shortly before the North-Vietnamese took over Saigon. You'll find the story of our community, our problems and our fears in this letter."

"How was it over there?"

"It was war, always war! God we suffered. Wallahi, we were scared! The chemical weapons poisoned the trees; people had chest pains and skin eruptions all over them. The skin ulcerations can be treated with injections, but your lungs are damaged permanently."

The Escape

The patriarch is quiet, fallen into sad thoughts. Thinking to comfort him, I say:

"Being foreign citizens, at least the young men in your community didn't have to worry about being drafted."

"Are you joking? Many were drafted anyway."

"And you couldn't do anything to stop it?"

The Imam replies with a hopeless smile, "Dear Madam, one doesn't fight with the army. . ."

He coughs, "Just as I had anticipated, Saigon became Ho-Chi-Minh City shortly after my call for help to Beijing. The communists occupied Saigon. They gave three days for the people to bring all their money to the State Bank and exchange it 100 to 1 for the new currency, the old one being useless. What madness! Can you imagine 17 million Vietnamese rushing from the most remote villages all the way to the banks in such a short time?"

"How did the Yemenite embassy in Beijing respond to your call for help?"

He takes out another document from his reliquary.

"Here's the reply. Thanks to Yemenite diplomats we're here. In 1976, the International Red Cross flew a plane packed full of our people from Saigon to Sanaa three times."

A Former "French" Soldier

A storm of anger interrupts the Imam's soft voice.

"But you forgot to tell the lady that when we arrived at the Sanaa airport the police took all our I.D. papers! They never returned them!"

This explosion comes out of the French-speaking mouth of Ali Abdallah Saleh, who until then had listened to our conversation without saying a word. The Imam is all the more disconcerted by the fact that he doesn't understand much French. He straightens his papers and leaves.

Ali, a sixty years old rover, was once a sailor on French merchant ships. During World War II he enrolled, more or less voluntarily, in the French navy. At the end of the fighting he was granted French citizenship. But he says that his passport burned in a fire in Saigon. "Ah, if only it hadn't burned. . ."

"Hundreds of French-Yemenites who were on French merchant ships like me, and who fought the war alongside the French like I did, now live the good life in Marseille thanks to their veterans' pension fund. I fought for nothing!"

The imam of Saigon's daughter-in-law and grandson were among the Yemenites exiled . . . in Yemen! When in Vietnam, the young woman learned English with the Americans but doesn't speak a word of Arabic.

When Saigon became Ho-Chi-Minh City in 1975, the Yemenite imam of Vietnam, Abdeirahman Ibn Hussein el-Khatibi, escaped the fate of the boat-people together with three hundred members of his community.

Ali, thinking he was finding freedom by fleeing Vietnam, today lives like a prisoner in the country of his ancestors. He hangs around the camp, biding time. He drags around in his old shoes, his baggy blue pyjamas, his melancholy and his nostalgia.

"Back when the French were there everything was booming in Vietnam. Business was good, they were building everywhere, crops were abundant. Ahh, what a good life. After they left everything changed. Towards the end we didn't think about working anymore. All we thought about was getting rid of the communists!"

Life is hopeless when all you have to fill your days are memories. At first the refugees were taken care of by the government. Now they have to manage on their own, but they don't manage well. They have a hard time finding work, even poorly-paid small jobs. Yet a family has to pay 500 rials a month to live in two tiny rooms of the camp.

A few lucky ones found their relatives in the villages of their ancestors, as soon as they arrived in Yemen. Others managed to open a restaurant in Sanaa or Hodeyda. But most of them are rotting in this dusty camp, sealed off by a wall of concrete and the wall of race, customs and language.

The verses of the Koran which the refugees droned out as children in the Saigon mosque help little in trying to learn the gutteral Arabic spoken by Yemenites. One by one the disoriented "Yem-Viets" have left the governmental schools which were open to them. Other luckier ones, though, benefit from the grants given to them by a rich Yemenite businessman and attend a school where Arabic and English are taught.

Refugees and Unveiled

Going bare-headed, their hair out in the open and dressed in the loose Vietnamese pyjama, women stranded by history on the strange planet of Yemen, run the risk of being jeered at. Women refugees have suffered more than the men in the sudden transition from Southeast Asia's tolerant Islam to the conservative Arab Islam. The women stay among themselves, sitting for hours in front of their doorways with blank stares, babies held against their breasts. On the road near the camp I ran into a small, old woman with a tight bun, dressed in dowdy looking Chinese black pants and a square-necked vest. This poor little thing, lost in the crowd of women blanketed in veils, unable to exchange even a smile with their covered faces, looked like the loneliest person in the world.

I visited the camp in Taiz in 1981. Since the "Yem-Viets'" arrival in 1976 only one man among them had married a Yemenite. No more than five or six refugee women had married local Yemenite men. The young women raised in Saigon shivered at the idea of being given away by their families to the boss-husband of a Yemenite village where they would have to slave away in the fields for the rest of their lives.

"We Had No Choice"

He was a musician and his name was Le Van Tram. He fought in American special forces units in Vietnam. Today with the name Seif Hassan Ali, his excellent English allows him to work in a Taiz bank. His wife, Nguyen Kim Ahn, who works in the same bank, was a secretary in Saigon for an American Office of Rural Pacification.

Neither Le, of remote Yemenite origins, nor Nguyen, Vietnamese and every inch a Buddhist, ever imagined that they would one day come to Yemen.

"We didn't have any choice. If we hadn't taken the plane the communists would have killed us."

Le and Nguyen live in the stifling heat of two tiny rooms with his mother and their three children. Their struggle to survive began in Vietnam, gun in hand, and continues in Yemen, pen in hand. Their letters are an endless string of pleas demanding the return of their confiscated documents. They persist, trying to speed up the request to emigrate to the West which has gotten stuck in the sands of bureaucracy.

While those in Taiz struggle to leave Yemen those who remained in Saigon try to move heaven and earth to fly away and escape.

"To Yemen, to the moon. Anywhere!"

Hell in the Sky

Wars and pending wars bring a flood of Yemenites back to their homeland.

Sixty year old Abdallah fled Ethiopia. His turban is lopsided, his glasses round, his wrinkles deep. He speaks in a very soft voice.

"I returned from Asmara in Eritrea, in the north of Ethiopia. In 1974, as soon as the Emperor was dethroned, the Liberation Front of Eritrea, long suppressed, awakened. The guerillas, slinking and creeping around, planted bombs in marketplaces, killed foreigners. I got scared. . ."

Abdallah, not long ago a merchant in the most ancient of empires, is today working in the most futuristic of buildings. The Yemen Airways building is a temple of modernity erect in the sky, higher and closer to God than any minarets in the capital.

For some, this Manhattan in Yemen symbolizes progress. For others these glass and steel skyscrapers are an insult to the brick and stucco towers standing in the ancient magical city of Sanaa. When I visited it, this avant-garde building planted in the middle of Arabia had no air conditioning!

"He Was A Good Emperor"

Standing in front of the tinted glass windows of the Yemen Airways building, Abdallah wipes his brow, clears his throat and continues his story.

"When I arrived in Ethiopia in 1935 at the age of 13, the Italians had just occupied the country. My father had been living with the King of Kings as far back as 1918. He had a shop in Asmara, but the majority of Yemenite merchants lived in the capital, Addis-Ababa. We liked the Italians since it was thanks to them that Ethiopia finally began to develop. In those days political parties didn't proliferate like locusts, destroying everything in their path!"

Abdallah cleans his glasses the better to see his memories.

"Being an emigrant, I was just on the fringes. I lived 40 years at the Negus's without speaking Ethiopia's language, Amharic. I barely know English. My Italian is limited to the 'troppo caro!" needed for merchants. My children went to the Arab school paid for by Yemenite merchants. In Asmara only one thing mattered, that there be peace in Ethiopia and that business keep rolling along. I prayed that there would be peace in Ethiopia, guided by the firm hand of Haile Selassie."

"Did you like him?" I ask.

"He was a despot. The people had no choice but to keep quiet and kiss his feet. He was a good emperor, though. Under his rule our property was protected!"

But life hadn't always been easy for Yemenite immigrants in the holy kingdom of the Lion of Judah. Abdallah confesses,

"Many Yemenites thought that the Revolution would bring liberalism and freedom to Ethiopia; they didn't get their capital out of the country on time. As soon as the emperor was overthrown the nationalists got into action. They told me, 'Abdallah, you only have right to a one bedroom house for you and your family.' Though I owned several houses, we had to squeeze ourselves into one of them."

The new sixty year old employee of Yemen Airways contemplates Sanaa through the bay window of the skyscraper.

"Goodbye, Ethiopia! Right before our eyes Marxism was born and a 3,000 year old empire died. I had to flee, for my children and for their future. I have good kids, God be praised! Not one of them has anything to do with politics. God be blessed!"

Like their brothers in Vietnam, the Yemenite merchants of Ethiopia asked Sanaa for help. The planes came to their rescue, flying from Yemen's capital across the Red Sea. Some emigrants managed to sell or save their possessions but others had to content themselves with saving the shirts on their backs and their own skins. Abdallah has never lost his common sense or his business sense:

"To be on the safe side my nephew stayed behind in Asmara. He lives in the only house we have left."

The uncle smiles ironically and tells the moral of his story:

"He who goes looking loses his return ticket, and, when he gets back he finds he's been fired, replaced by an Ethiopian!"

They Return From the Hot Spots

Yemenite emigrants have returned from many other hot spots around the Red Sea. Among them were shopkeepers from Somalia who had grown tired of the shaky politics, and businessmen from Djibouti who left in 1977 after that country's independence. But with their entrepreneurial zeal it would take little to encourage them to leave yet again on new voyages and new business adventures!

How many busy Yemenite bees are there now on foreign soil? There were about one million or more in Saudi Arabia and the Arab Gulf countries—but these numbers moved just as these emigrants had, coming and going, often crossing the borders illegally. Most recently, in 1990, as a result of the Gulf crisis following the invasion of Kuwait by Iraq, half a million Yemenites in Saudi Arabia returned to Yemen.

The most stable communities (thanks to the stability of their host countries) are in the United States and England, each of which have 20,000 to 30,000 immigrants, perhaps more. There are about

10,000 in Kenya and about 1,000 in France. The communities of Ethiopia (once 20,000 to 25,000), Somalia (10,000 to 15,000) and Southeast Asia (numbers unknown) have shrunken drastically.

Nahema the African

Good humored Nahema Fadel, daughter of a Yemenite merchant and an African woman, didn't leave her native Sudan because of political upheaval. Attracted by the prospect of a good job, she chose to go and discover the country of her ancestors.

"Since the Revolution, anyone with an education has had a chance for a better life in Yemen. Offices, schools, and businesses are opening up everywhere. Out of the thousands of Yemenites settled in the Sudan, the majority have already returned."

Even though Nahema is satisfied with her work, she doesn't suffer any the less for being an exile in Yemen, "the jailor of women" as she puts it.

"I am Black. Often people think I'm a foreigner which has its advantages. It allows me to come and go as I please. But as soon as they find out I'm a Yemenite citizen they don't smile anymore . . . I'm twenty-two and at this age it's unacceptable to live here and be single. My parents stayed in Sudan and I live with my uncle who has one thing in mind—to have me married. But I have only one idea in my head—to study."

Nahema is a secretary in one of the offices of the Emigrants' Association, a big building, modern, but built in traditional Yemenite style and sited at the very edge of Sanaa.

Perpetually on the Move

All these personal accounts from Saudi Arabia, Vietnam, Ethiopia and Sudan, reveal to what extent Yemenites have always been on the move. Be it in times ancient or modern, they took to the road or the sea, emigrating in waves large and small. In ancient times the decline of their civilization propelled them onto trails in the Old World, towards Syria and, especially, Mesopotamia. In the 7th century of the Christian era they enlisted by the thousands, armed and with horses, in the Prophet's armies for the great glory of Allah. Later, fleeing poverty and the cruelty of Imams, they scattered everywhere.

Since the country opened up in 1970, more of them now leave than ever before. Those departing today hope to bring back someday enough money to develop their villages, to build houses, to settle onto their cushions and to find wives for their beds.

Until the early 1970's the emigrants had been left to fend for themselves, to get along as best they could. Their only support abroad was from a little nucleus of Yemenites, often from the same village. Their first attempt at organizing took place only as recently as 1976 when delegates from nearly all the world's emigrant Yemenite communities attended a conference in Sanaa. Their creation was the Emigrants' Association whose 26 branches now cover most of the globe.

Two Americans in Sanaa

A Yemenite of Brooklyn, New York, tells about the perpetual migrations of his countrymen with humor and pride:

"When I saw the Americans land on the moon for the first time I thought it was wonderful, but in a way I was disappointed. I was expecting the astronauts to be met by a Yemenite!"

Mohammed Dailam re-turbanned and re-skirted himself to take a vacation in his home country. I had met him at the Emigrants' Association in Sanaa. He stammers in the little bit of English that he knows:

"In the U.S. I work twelve hours a day making 1,000 bucks a month. I send cash to Yemen. I've got an American passport now, but I wouldn't mind coming back for good if it were stable here and I could find a good job with good money."

His friend Mohsen Al Roobat also boasts American citizenship and a smile of dentures "made in the USA." The whiteness of his teeth contrasts with the green teeth of the multitudes of quat chewers. He wears a jacket in pink and baby blue. It's been seven years since Mohsen returned to Yemen. Today, he passes by the Emigrants' Association "just to say hello." But the real reason that every month he feels compelled to leave his house perched on a mountainside is to collect his $290 social security check at the American Embassy. His English is better than Mohammed's.

"America's a good country. What's missing is security. In Yemen you feel protected, there you're scared. Here, there isn't a window between a taxi driver and his passenger like in New York. And yet in Yemen we all have guns!"

"One night in Brooklyn there was a gang of us in the street. Some black men shot at us. Three Yemenites were killed. The police didn't even go after the killers . . . When I complained about it the cop told me, 'Hey guy, where do you think you are? They never found the guy who shot Kennedy; you think I'm going to find the guy who shot three Arabs in Brooklyn?!"

But in spite of all this Mohsen still admires his second homeland. The American example is an inspiration to him:

"Democracy here in Yemen wouldn't be bad. . ."

"The Homeland": A Monthly Magazine

The communities of Yemenite workers in the West stay among themselves. In Brooklyn as in Yemen the men stay together and the women are hardly freer than they were in Yemen, at least among the first generation of emigrants. Isolated by language barriers and cooped up by tradition, the women live their modest lives, with the housework, shopping, kids, gossip and T.V.

The emigrants have their mosques, their restaurants, and their grocery stores are redolent with the sweet smell of spices and seasonings. In the shops the intoxicating perfumes and full candy jars are set among the newspapers from Yemen, the Arabic publications, the pictures of saints and Koranic verses. Under little plastic domes, which replace the old-fashioned ceramic ones, one can find over-sweetened sticky golden cakes. They cling to the fingers of these exiles like the memories of their village feasts, their marriages and births, back there, back home, back then . . .

But Yemenites, separated by oceans and continents, are linked by something other than just those sweet-shop reminiscences. It's the monthly magazine, "The Homeland" (*El Watan*), published in Sanaa by the Emigrants' Association. This attractive magazine has a world-wide circulation of 15,000.

A True Tale

It is rare for a Yemenite emigrant to marry a western woman. But that doesn't stop love taking its course.

Allah decided that one fine day at the end of World War II, a Yemenite working man, named Ahmed Nagy, would meet a French working woman, named Rosa Wardenski, and fall in love with her. The romance began in 1945 in the Manufrance factory of Saint-Etienne and ended in 1950 in Bordeaux, where Ahmed worked on the docks. Out of their passion Ali and Saida were conceived, in love, but out of wedlock.

Above: In 1950, Ahmed Nagy, docker in Bordeaux, France (wearing a Turkish hat in the photograph), kidnapped his two children, then aged four and five, from their French-Polish mother. He took them with him to Yemen where the children would live a tale of a thousand and one episodes.

Left: Saida and Ali in 1955, at the court of the King of Yemen.

No, 3512/22/H

بسم الله الرحمن الرحيم

Taiz, Le 17 November 1955.

Madame Rosa Wardenski,

    Après les compliments- en me
referant a votre lettre du 19 Septembre
1955, que vous avez envoyée à Sa Majeste
L'imam Roi Du Yemen, concernant vos ieux
enfants Ali et Saida, je porte a votre
connaissance que vos enfants jouisset de
la meilleure sante et se trouvent dans
les meilleurs conditions, vu la grane
sympathie et la bonne bienveillance que
Sa Majeste les accorde. Pour vous
rassurer je suis tres heureux de vous e
envoyer ci-inclus une photographie ceux,
recemment prise.

    Je porte avotre connaissance
encore si vous desirez venir à Taiz,
YEMEN, pour les visiter, qu'il N'y a
aucune objection à condition que ce soit
pour une periode limitée. Dans ce c cette
lettre est considere'e comme votre isa
d'entre'e au Yemen, etje vous sujjer de
venir par la voie de Djibouti, Cote
Francaise Des Somalis où il vous sera
possible de prendre l'avion Yémenite
qui voyage regulierement tout les samedis
entre Taiz et Djibouti.

    Il serait preferable que
vous nous informiez par telegramme du jour
de votre arrivée à Djibouti pour vous
faciliter votre rentrée par le dit avion
à Taiz. Il serait encore preferable si
vous arrivez à Djibouti avant samedi
matin le jour du depart de l'avion.

    Veuillez Madame accepter
nos salutations distinguees.

Le Secretaire.

حضرة المدام روزا واردنسكي المحترمة

بعد التحية ـ وبالاشارة الى رسالتك تاريخ
١٩ سبتمبر سنة ١٩٥٥ المرفوعة لحضرة
صاحب الجلالة الملك المعظم بخصوص ولدي يك
علي وسيدة ٠ احيطك علما بان ولدي يك يتمتعان
باحسن الصحة وفي حالة جيدة جدا لما
يسبغه عليهما حضرة صاحب الجلالة الملك
المعظم من جميل عطف وحسن رعاية ٠ ولطمئنك
عليهما يسرني ان ابعث اليك طيه بصورة
فتوغرافية اخذت حديثا ٠

واود احاطتك علما ايضا بانه اذ اتوفرت
لديك الرغبة في الوصول الى تعز اليمن بقصد
زيارتهما فلا مانع بذلك لمدة محدودة ٠
وفي هذا ٠ الحالة يعتبر هذا الكتـــاب
تصريحا لك بالد خول الى اليمن والخــرج
عليك في حالة عزمك على الحضور ان يكون
حضورك من فرنسا الى دجيبوتي في الصومال
الفرنسي حيث يمكنك الركوب على طـائـرة
يمنية تابعة لخطوط الطيران اليمنيــة
وتقوم طائراتنا هذه بـرحلة جوية واحدة
الى دجيبوتي يوم السبت من كل اسبوع ٠
ويستحسن ان تعليمينا عن موعد
وصولك الى دجيبوتي لعمل الترتيبات اللازمة
بركو بك على احدى طائراتنا الى تعز كمـا
يستحسن ان يكون وصولك الى دجيبوتي
قبل صباح يوم السبت من اى اسبوع ٠
واقبلي تحياتي ٠

المسكرتير

Because of their blue eyes and blond hair the children would later live in Yemen a tale of a thousand and one episodes.

One day in 1950 Ali and Saida, who lived with their mother, were taken by their father to go three times around on the merry-go-round. Three times around and away they went . . . never to be seen again.

The father-kidnapper told his children that their mother had thrown the three of them, the girl, the boy and the father, out of the house for good. When you're four and five years old you cry, but you believe what your daddy tells you.

In 1955 after five years of searching and tears, Rosa found out through the stories that traveled with the Yemenite sailors, that Ali and Saida were living in Taiz in the King of Yemen's palace. She

---

Taiz, November 17, 1955.

Madame Rosa Wardenski,

Greetings. I address myself to your letter dated September 19, 1955 which you sent to His Majesty, The King of Yemen, regarding your two children, Ali and Saida. I want to inform you that your children are in the best of health and circumstances, as His Majesty gives the best of care and attention to them. I am very happy to be able to send you a recently-taken photograph of the two.

I would also like to inform you that if you would like to come to Taiz, Yemen, to visit them that there are no objections, granted that it be of short duration. This letter will be considered your entrance visa to Yemen and I suggest that you come by way of Djibouti, the French coast of Somalia, where it would be possible for you to take the Yemenite plane which goes from Djibouti to Taiz every Saturday.

It would be best that you inform us by telegram of the date of your arrival so that we may facilitate your travel by the said plane to Taiz. It would be most preferable for you to arrive in Djibouti before Saturday morning, the day of the plane's departure.

With best regards,

The Secretary

wrote to the Imam Ahmed. "The Sword of Islam" answered from the height of his royal cushions and his absolute power with a letter and a photograph of the children. He invited Rosa to his faraway castle but not once did he suggest that he would return the little stolen children to their mother. (She did not go to Yemen.)

Today, Rosa, married to a second Yemenite and the mother of 14 more children, still lives in Bordeaux. She remembers that she had a mixed feeling of relief and fear.

"I was happy to know that they were alive, but I was afraid of what could still happen to them! News continued to come to me until 1960, and, then, nothing more! The Revolution had begun in Yemen. In 1970 the International Red Cross informed me that Ali and Saida had been killed in the Revolution."

From what she was told Rosa figured out that Ali and Saida had probably been killed in 1962 when the palace was seized by the Revolutionaries.

But the truth was that Ali and his sister were alive and well. When I met him, Ali was in charge of public relations for the Ministry of Information in Sanaa. He was also a member of the Yemenite National Theatre troup where he displayed all his talents as a singer and a comedian.

He says he vaguely remembers a childhood voyage accompanied by his father and sister from Bordeaux to Taiz, via Marseille, Port-Said, Djibouti and Aden. He has only a hazy image of going up from Aden to Taiz along a rocky, dusty trail in a car, rattling along from mountain to mountain. Every mountain pass was guarded by soldiers with big turbans and big guns.

Yet he clearly remembers the horror he felt when he discovered what poverty was with his innocent child eyes. It was in September 1950, a month of great famine in Yemen. Surrounded by strange skinny people in rags the two little French children screamed in terror.

"Bring Them to Me"

The Imam Ahmed's men who were watching the road near Taiz and the royal castle, summoned the father to stop his car. The curious clustered around the car. They were fascinated by the automobile, but especially the children. These angels in shorts and a little skirt enraptured them like flowers enrapture bees. Their eyes danced over the children, their dress, and their blond hair.

Perplexed by what he had heard, the Imam thundered out the orders,

"Bring them to me!"

The royal guards brought Ali and Saida before the King. The father could say nothing or the King would have had his head. The King made his decision; the children would stay in the royal court and their father would only see them once a month, on Fridays (the Muslim Sunday).

The monarch had set his eye on Ali:

"You are my favored one!"

The Imam's fifteen-year-old adopted son only had eyes for Saida,

"I want this doll. When she grows up I will marry her!"

The two little captives left behind their French pleated skirts and short pants for the clothes and Arabic language of Yemen. Later they would be given a fine Yemenite style education. Ali would practice martial arts, swimming and acrobatics on horseback.

The palace's nannies assigned to the blond children were slaves. The Imam had perhaps 300 slaves, men and women, black and white. His white captives had been stolen as children, often far, far away from Yemen, many of them sold and resold. Considered valuable, they were very expensive.

Once watched over by the King's guards, today Saida is watched over by her husband, a guard of the Republic. In Sanaa she lives the simple life of a plump Yemenite woman. The only traces left of France are her blue eyes.

In 1962, after the Imam was killed, the civil war between the monarchists and the republicans started. Saida's father took her from the palace and hid her in a village. The girl was 15 years old at the time. She had spent 11 years in the shadow of Ahmed the Djinn.

"But we were pampered," she told me, "especially Ali. My brother was the Imam's darling."

The former favorite added:

"But I was stubborn, feisty, and undisciplined!"

Sweetened Condensed Milk

But the despot liked the little cherub's strong character. He was rarely punished for his tantrums.

One day when, in direct rebellion to religious law, Ali refused to pray, he was only deprived of the pocket money he used to buy candy and the sweetened condensed milk, which was a very, very rare luxury in Yemen.

The monarch made a gift to him of one of his finest horses, a present he hadn't given even his own children. At age 11 the Imam's little favorite was even given horsepower—an American automobile.

The Imam Ahmed who was all giving to his favorite had no such tenderness for his people. Ali still remembers all of this with indignation,

"Every Friday the executioner's sword sliced off two heads in the public square. The guilty were usually common criminals, but to scare the people the King made political prisoners out of them. He used hand signals to sentence them. When Ahmed, sitting on his cushion, tapped his palm against his knee, it meant he was very angry. If he stroked his beard it meant that he wanted to think it over. When he pinched his chin between his index and middle finger it meant that the sentence was one month to five years in prison, depending on his mood. But if he put his wrist on his knee and waved those same two fingers stuck together, back and forth, it meant death."

The Imam Collapses

Over the 11 years he spent in the palace Ali's knowledge, if not his wisdom, grew. One day in 1962, the King decided to send his favorite together with three of his own sons to have piloting lessons in Germany. The young boys, all excited about this adventure, were settling into their seats when the Imam suddenly appeared on the runway and commanded them to come out of the plane.

"You ingrates! You haven't come to see me. You will not leave on this plane until you have bowed your heads and shown me some respect!"

The Imam's voice snapped like a whip, the sons of Ahmed obeyed and kissed the royal hand. The favored one just made a short bow. He was 16 years old and couldn't stand the tyrant anymore.

Ali can't help but laugh today at his own insolence. He chuckles,

"The old man was scarlet with rage and his morphine addict eyes were popping out of his head. He avenged himself. He gave orders for the plane to leave without me!"

In 1961 a few months before his unsuccessful departure for

Germany, Ali had escorted the Imam to the hospital in Hodeyda to pay a visit to one of the King's nephews. This time the Revolutionaries, always watching and waiting, didn't miss their target. The Imam was to die the next year of his wounds.

Ali hasn't forgotten anything of that unforgettable day.

"It all happened so fast. The lights went out! Shots were fired! The Imam collapsed. His guards killed two of the assassins but the third one escaped. I thought the Imam was lying at my feet dead, but Ahmed was such a good actor that he managed to get up in spite of the eight bullets in him, clutch my arm, whispering in my ear, 'Ali, if anyone asks you, tell him that their Imam was invincible. Tell them that the djinns protected me!"

The favorite witnessed the last convulsions of the last potentate of Yemen,

"He was in so much pain. Only morphine relieved him. He constantly begged for it. Towards the end we just filled the needles with water."

After the death of the despot in 1962, Ali enlisted himself in the Republican army. The blond boy once kidnapped by his father, then by the King of Yemen, took up arms against the monarchists. The fighting was fierce. Yemen thundered, convulsed and bled. At last the Republic had won. From now on Yemenites would be able to have medicine and eat, laugh, dance, sing, read and write.

Again Love In Another Land

Ali then left for the land of Lebanon. There he would continue his quest for knowledge and study. He was a handsome boy with thick curly blond hair and deep, spectacular blue eyes. Ali was a charmer but beneath he had a strong character, acute intelligence and a great deal of insolence.

Having been graced with a grant from the USSR the young man left for Moscow. But he had the unfortunate idea of adding to his university stipend the money he earned through the black market. Ali, Ahmed-the-Djinn's favorite, was forced to leave the university to go to jail. There he discovered that the prisons of the Soviet Union where he rotted for a year weren't any better than the dungeons of Yemen. But like his father in France, Ali would find love in exile. He married a Russian woman. The darling boy of yore became a papa.

Back in Sanaa, Ali discovered yet another truth—that the borders of the modern "enlightened" USSR were as hermetically sealed as were those of the feudal kingdom of Ahmed. He moved heaven and desert dunes to try and find a way for his wife and daughter to leave Russia and join him in Yemen. All in vain. Discouraged by years of futile efforts he finally decided to find himself another wife.

Then in 1979 the incredible story of Ali would suddenly become a modern fairy tale like the Arab tales which never end, the story teller always inventing yet another episode. In Ali's story the invisible radio waves of the French radio station "France-Inter" would replace the flying carpets of yore. While on assignment in Yemen the French journalist Dominique Guilhot sought the help of the Ministry of Information. He was put under Ali's wing. This is how he learned Ali's life story.

When he returned to Paris in the cold month of December, the journalist made a special broadcast on France-Inter. Ali's mother Rosa Wardenski will never forget her stupefaction.

"I was watching television when the phone rang. It was fate on the phone. My neighbor who knew my story, had just heard Dominique Guilhot on the radio. She was frantic, 'I think they're talking about you, Rosa, and your children Ali and Saida. You have to write France-Inter!"

But Rosa couldn't wait,

"Write? Are you out of your mind! I went straight to the phone. It really was my children they were talking about!"

The true fairy tale continues.

In May 1980 Ali jetted across the sky from Sanaa to Paris. France-Inter had organized a meeting and paid for Rosa's trip from Bordeaux to Paris.

"In the airport I recognized him immediately, even though it had been 30 years since my little one was stolen from me!"

In front of the press and the photographers—who for once seemed touched—Ali slipped a silver Yemenite necklace over his mother's neck. Dominique Guilhot brought them to the studios of France-Inter where they were the overwhelmed and overwhelming stars of a radio show.

"What language do you speak with your son?" I asked Rosa.

"On the radio show we had interpreters but when we're alone we usually speak . . . Russian and Polish! As you know my parents were Poles and Ali learned Russian in the Soviet Union. I also learned a little Arabic with the two Yemenite fathers of my 16 children.

In March 1981 Rosa flew off to Yemen where she discovered the country whose charm and hospitality her men had told her so much about.

"I cried when I saw my daughter. Saida cried too. More than anything she wanted to come back with me to France, but she couldn't just leave her husband and children behind."

However, Saida was soon to go on a visit to France where she had been born.

Her life, like Yemen's, tells of the brutal encounter between an ancient culture and the modern world. Her memories, like Yemen's, are those of excruciating separations and, for the fortunate, intense, overwhelming reunifications.

Sunset in Djibla.

Some emigrants use these colorful painted metal boxes as trunks. The peasant women—who don't travel—use the big ones to keep their clothes and other paraphernalia.

Sanaa.

SAUDI ARABIA

RED
SEA

ASIR

TIHAMA

SAADA

KHAMER

RAIDA

AMRAN

HAJJA

SANAA

Yeme

MARIB

BAYHAN

NISAB

HODAYDA

DHAMAR

ZABID

DATHINA

DJIBLA

IBB

DALA

SHUQRA

AL MUKA

TAIZ

ABYAN

ZINJIBAR

ADEN

ETHIOPIA

STRAITS OF BAB-EL-MAND

In the **Tihama plain** along the Red Sea, desert and fertile land alterna
The climate is torrid, moist, and in some places insalubrious.

The **middle plateaus** are parallel to the Red Sea coast at an altitu
between 550m and 1650 m. Terraced crops. The climate is temperat

The **high plateaus** are part of the chain of mountains crossing Yem
from north to south—the highest peak of which is also the highest in t
Middle East: 3760m. Sanaa is built at 2350m. The climate is extreme

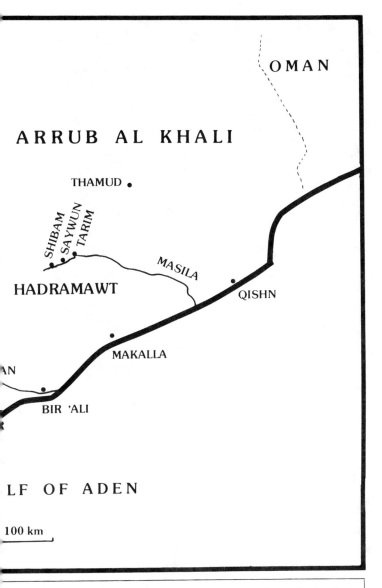

OMAN

ARRUB AL KHALI

THAMUD •

SHIBAM
SAYWUN
TARIM

HADRAMAWT

MASILA

QISHN

•
MAKALLA

•AN

•
BIR 'ALI

LF OF ADEN

100 km

The **eastern plateaus** start not far from Sanaa and end up in the Arrub l-Khali desert. The more one goes towards the east, the more the climate ets hot and dry.

The climate on the **sea coasts** is hot and moist. At the southern end of e Red Sea, Yemen controls the Straits of Bab-El-Mandeb. On the uthern coast, the port of Aden holds a strategic position.

nportant cities: Sanaa (political capital), Aden (economic capital), aiz, Hodayda.

Wedding night in Sanaa. It's only an illusion: the candles are on a tray carried by one of the groom's friends behind the boy's head.

GLOSSARY

Caravanserai: hostel for caravans where the travelers were put up together with their camels, horses, etc.

Hamam: public bath

Hegira: Islamic era starting in the year 622 A.D.

Henna: extract from the leaves of a small tree used to dye the hair and decorate the body—henna is color red

Khol: natural product used as eye-maker in the Near and Middle East

Mousharabieh: wooden lattice-work placed in front of a window in moslem countries which allows one to see without being seen

Muezzin: the man who calls the Moslems for prayer five times a day from the top of the mosque minaret

Quat: the Yemenites' drug of preference—a plant grown year round in shrubs on Yemen mountain slopes

Ramadan: 9th month of the moslem lunar year. During the month of Ramadan the moslems fast from dawn to dusk

Rial: (Yemenite): 12 rials = 1 US dollar (in 1991)

Sheikh: Arabic word meaning literally "chief", either tribal or religious

Laurence Deonna, of Swiss nationality, is an international free-lance journalist and photographer for many and diverse journals at home and abroad.

Her work has led her to all the continents (except Antarctica), but it is the Middle East, with its ancient civilizations, its ever-constant turmoil, and the "feminine condition" so different from that in the West, that has been her major "beat."

Among her works is a book on Arab women, a personal record of her adventures around the world, *From the Bottom of My Suitcase*, and *The War with Two Voices* (Three Continents, 1989), interviews with Egyptian and Israeli women, whose men (husbands, sons, brothers) had fought each other (this work was awarded the UNESCO Peace Education Prize in 1987).